When Your Nephew Joins the Moonies...

Also by Richard E. Wentz

▼

Why Do People Do Bad Things
in the Name of Religion?

Religion in the New World

The Contemplation of Otherness

Saga of the American Soul

"When Your Nephew Joins the Moonies"

And Other Letters to the Christians of St. Woebegone's

Richard E. Wentz

COWLEY PUBLICATIONS
Cambridge, Massachusetts

FORWARD MOVEMENT PUBLICATIONS
Cincinnati, Ohio

Published in the United States of America
by Cowley Publications, a division of the Society
of St. John the Evangelist, in conjunction with Forward
Movement Publications. No portion of this book may be reproduced,
stored in or introduced into a retrieval system, or transmitted, in
any form or by any means—including photocopying—without
the prior written permission of Cowley Publications, except
in the case of brief quotations embodied in critical
articles and reviews.

Library of Congress Cataloging-in-Publication Data
Wentz, Richard E.
When your nephew joins the Moonies : and other letters to the
Christians of St. Woebegone's / Richard E. Wentz.
p. cm.
Includes bibliographical references.
ISBN 1-56101-015-4 (alk. paper)
1. Christian life—Anglican authors. 2. Imaginary letters. I. Title.
BV4501.2.W425 1990
248.4'83—dc20   90-43816

Excerpt from "Choruses from 'The Rock'" in T. S. Eliot, *The Complete
Poems and Plays*, copyright 1971 by Esmé Valerie Eliot, reprinted by
permission of Harcourt Brace Jovanovich.

Excerpts from "The Cocoon" and "A Masque of Mercy" in *The Poetry
of Robert Frost*, Edward C. Lathem, ed., copyright 1979, reprinted by
permission of Henry Holt and Company.

This book is printed on acid-free paper and was produced in the
United States of America.

Cowley Publications
980 Memorial Drive
Cambridge, Massachusetts 02138

To my friends
in the Church of the Epiphany, Tempe,
and St. Paul's Church, Payson—all of them saints
seldom as woebegone as I.

Acknowledgments

I want to acknowledge the constant encouragement of my wife, Yvonne, who usually helps me with my proof reading and reminds me that it is important to be understood. She is always a beautiful gadfly for apologetic necessity.

Of course, the Rev. Fathers Carl G. Carlozzi and Richard M. George, Jr., of All Saints' Church, Phoenix, bear some responsibility for this book. They invited me to do two series of four lectures for the people of All Saints'. Inasmuch as they provided no further directives, they gave license to my imagination and the generation of these letters. I have since received absolution from them on numerous occasions. I wish to acknowledge here my friendship and gratitude to these faithful priests of the church.

I must include a special word of appreciation to the friendly advice and encouragement of Cynthia Shattuck, Editorial Director for Cowley Publications.

Richard E. Wentz

Contents

Introduction
1

"When Others Don't Act Like Christians"
7

"When Christianity Doesn't Make Sense"
23

"When You No Longer Know What Faith Means"
39

"When Your Nephew Joins the Moonies"
55

"When You're All Stressed Out"
73

"When Your Business Has No Time for Ethics"
93

"When Prayer Seems Like Wishful Thinking"
109

"When Money Seems to Talk Too Much"
129

"When You Think 'When You're Dead,
You're Dead' " .
145

Introduction

These letters are directed to members of the church in a post-Christian, post-modern world. In Arizona, the Republican party recently adopted a proposition claiming America as a Christian nation and dedicating itself to the nurture of that conviction. Thirty-five years ago that pronouncement would have gone largely unnoticed. In 1989 the furor of opposition has forced the Republicans to reconsider their imprudence. Although the modern secularist goes rabid at the suggestion, I hasten to add that, for most of our history, America was indeed a Christian nation. Not all people were Christian, and no official documents stated unequivocally that Christianity had licensed status. But the constitution of the public mind of the nation was fundamentally Christian; and public addresses and proceedings made note of that fact.

Since the early nineteen-sixties we have begun to be aware of the radically pluralistic character of American society. And, along with the pluralism, there is a growing secularism that makes the church an alien remnant of an age of credulity. Some years ago now, Martin Marty called attention to the fact that we live under the twofold sign of increased religiousness and increased secularity. That is probably a valid observation, but right now the secularist mentality has control of our educational philosophy and institutions, and is in great favor with those who influence the

1

direction of our morality and culture. Secularism is the mass mind, the collective mind, the mind turned in upon itself, with nothing to draw us out of misguided self-exaltation. In some sense, this is a world gone bonkers, in which the images and stories of the small screen that come to pass seem more real than life itself. It is a perplexed world, and sometimes none are more perplexed than those Christians who try to hang onto some God-given sanity even as they are sucked into the murk of greed and consumerism.

Christian churches that owe much of their personality to the heritage of the sixteenth century have not had an easy time of it in this post-Christian world. These churches have frequently been referred to as the "mainline." They are churches like the Presbyterian, the Episcopal, the American Baptist, the United Methodist, and the United Church of Christ. Even the Lutherans, who are strongly confessional, and the Roman Catholics have suffered in these latter days. The churches that have grown, making Marty's comment about increased religiousness viable, are those that give the people what they want. They are the institutions that offer a slick "how to" message for a people dedicated to the sanctification of success, greed, and happiness. To the extent that these groups are Christian, they package formulas for immediate salvation. And they have been joined by numerous cults and "new religions" in their response to the demands of modernity.

In such a world as this, St. Anne's and St. Michael and All Angels have a rough time of it. The public is not interested, it seems, in the mediated salvation of the Catholic tradition of Christianity. St. Anne's becomes St. Woebegone's—slow in its growth, small in membership, and populated by those who cast longing eyes at the successful lives of others who attend the 6,000-member First Assembly of God, and at the smug hedonism of their secular friends.

It is to the members of St. Woebegone's that these letters are written. They are offered in great deference to that rich epistolary tradition that goes back to St. Paul's "letters to the young churches" of apostolic Christianity. The message to perplexed Christians is a simple one: do not be anxious about your life, what you shall eat or what you shall drink; do not be anxious about to-morrow. Hunker down. The tempest rages, but there is a stilling of the waters. There is peace, but it is not the peace we demand. Live quietly. Do what you can do. Don't fall head over heels in love with the gaudy promises of a worn-out world. Just fall in love and go to eucharist as you go to your own table. Just go. Live in common prayer. Learn a bit of sacrifice. And, for God's sake, laugh. Laugh at the pretensions of those who take themselves so seriously. Laugh at yourself. Above all, laugh at yourself.

What better way to deal with this business of hunkering down than in letters shared with people with pressing concerns, churned up and washed ashore as the storms threaten and thunder. So you think you are suffering, says St. Paul, the great writer of letters. Well—"I consider that the sufferings of this present time are not worth comparing with the glory that is to be revealed to us." What is suffering but the disorganization of a world that is not sufficiently aware of the coinherence, the personal coinherence, of all being. Nothing wills its own existence, but is created out of nothing. There is a power and a meaning that are greater than all attempts to fashion the universe in our own image. There is power at the heart of the universe, but it is power that is shared mind—the mind we have *among* ourselves. "For the creation waits with eager longing for the revealing of the sons of God." Suffering is what we must endure in the present order of self-exaltation. The people have many problems, many questions, and serious misgivings. Let them tell us. Let them tell their stories in all honesty.

The Catholic tradition of Christianity must be prepared to lose its life for the sake of the truth of the Gospel it nourishes and mediates. The tradition must not sell its soul to the religiosity of an age that is intent upon self-gratification and justification. The modern world has transformed much of human religiousness, including *Christian* religiousness, into a brand of heavenly utilitarianism. By this I mean the individual desire to pursue goals defined and plotted according to the designs of the ordinary mind—whether those goals are this-worldly or other-worldly. Heavenly utilitarianism is the scheme of assured salvation that satisfies our desire for rewards here and in "the hereafter." And, of course, the forms of institutionalization in the modern world have been shaped by this utilitarianism. Therefore, the churches become anxious about their tomorrows and struggle to find acceptable language and motivations that can be used to save their own lives by promising the people what they want to hear. We hear talk of stewardship and evangelism, not in the biblical or apostolic sense of them, but in frantic concern for the sanctification of spiritual greed that often takes place in the churches. Recent efforts to promote tithing are neither biblical nor apostolic, but a question of expedience, and the worst piety is that which tries to lay guilt upon people for not conforming to the demands of the churches for self-preservation.

The question we face as members of churches like St. Woebegone's is: how do we live by the truth of the Gospel in a world which has little place for it—in its quotidian of work, pleasure, and religion? How do we sing the Lord's song in a strange land? How do we preserve this truth for the rebuilding of the social and cultural order? How do we preserve it without trying to *possess* it or use it to justify our own whimsical religiousness? These are not easy questions. They are not easy to address.

We worry about the loss of the world we have known. Even the lukewarm members of churches, and those who are not troubled at all by membership, like to know that the old guideposts have not been struck down. The person who has little concern for keeping the law likes to know that it's there. The person who attends to the eucharist only rarely is most likely to be chagrined when a daughter turns on to Scientology or gives up on a business management degree in order to major in religious studies.

I hope these letters help us to appreciate the complexity of the issues and to discover the grace to smile as we learn to accept the world, to take life as it comes. This continues to be a world where crucifixions take place, often in the name of religion. But it is also a world intersected by the compassionate presence of Him who reminds us that we are more than we think, that the time will be redeemed. And that is worth a smile and a hearty toast!

"When Others Don't Act Like Christians"

Dear Virginia,

What a coincidence! Three letters this past week—all of them on the same subject. Yours is very special, but I won't quote it here, simply because I thought it would be helpful for you to see your concerns expressed in someone else's words. Here is a point of view, familiar to you, but not from someone you know. The letter reads:

"I have been a member of St. Anne's-by-the-Butte for more than twenty-five years. During that time I have seen rectors who have been little less than dictators. I have seen others who did little more than try to please the wealthier parish-

7

ioners—those with power! But I've told myself that the church isn't the rector. Rectors come and go. It's the Body of Christ that's important. So I've hung on.

"However, during the past two years St. Anne's has been in for rough times. We've had some real division in the congregation. It has finally gotten to me. I don't understand how people who call themselves Christians can display as much hatred as they do. It's impossible to keep your faith in the midst of hypocrisy. I'm finding it very difficult to be part of organized religion. I don't know if it's worth it, or whether I can handle it anymore."

I know the woman who wrote that letter very well. She reminds me so very much of you. And St. Anne's-by-the-Butte reminds me very much of St. Woebegone's, and many another woeful parish. So let me try to speak to your concerns by replying to her letter.

First, let me say that I am always surprised at people who are surprised by the behavior of other people. I am not surprised by hatred in the church or anywhere else in the world. I am not surprised by what the woman called 'hypocrisy.' I never expect anything else; and all I expect the church in this world to be is a crucified body that God raises again and again from the dead. All I expect of the church is that people who hate should be humbled by their hatred, that they should be reconciled to those they hate. Now, I don't believe that humility happens just because I tell myself that I should be humble, that I should be reconciled to those with whom I'm in disharmony. Being humble is never the result of trying to be humble. A person who tries to be humble is a bit nauseating, an insult to God, and very trying to my patience. Humility, like forgiveness and reconciliation, is a gift. It is the result of continuing to live in the broken body where God's grace can overcome my weakness, my attachments, my stubbornness.

If I separate myself from the broken body of Christ, I will find it difficult to share in the resurrection it receives. If I separate myself, I am saying, "I know what people should be like. I know how they should behave. And if they don't behave that way, I will go and be righteous by myself." You see, we cannot be righteous by ourselves. One of the most effective of principles in the broken body of Christ is the discovery that it's very difficult to judge someone else.

In the writings of the desert fathers, there's the story of Abba Moses who was asked to attend a council called to deal with a brother who had committed a fault of some kind. Abba Moses refused to go. Finally the priest sent someone to say to him, "Everyone is waiting for you. Please come. Hurry!" So Abba Moses got up, took a leaking jug, filled it with water, and went to the council. When the others went out to greet him, they saw the leaking jug and asked, "What is this, Father?" The old man said to them, "My sins run out behind me, and I do not even see them, yet today I am coming to judge the errors of another." When the brothers heard him, they dismissed the council and forgave the brother.

In the same way, another brother came to put a case before old Abba Moses. "Here is a man who beats his servant because of a fault he's committed; what should the servant say?" Abba Moses answered, "If he is a good servant, he should say,

'Forgive me, I have sinned.'" The brother asked, "Nothing else? Is that all?" The old man replied, "No, because from the moment he takes upon himself responsibility for the affair and says, 'I have sinned,' immediately the Lord will have mercy on him. The aim in all these things is not to judge one's neighbor. For truly, when the hand of the Lord caused all the first-born in the land of Egypt to die, no house was without its dead." The brother asked, "What does this mean?" Abba Moses answered, "If we are on watch to see our own faults, we shall not see those of our neighbor. It is folly for a man who has a dead person in his house to leave him there and go to weep over his neighbor's dead. To die to one's neighbor is this: To bear your own faults and not to pay attention to others, wondering whether they are good or bad."

Even in the Epistle of James—that New Testament book which often seems so out of place because of its emphasis on justification by works—James says, "He that speaks evil against a brother or judges his brother, speaks evil against the law and judges the law. But if you judge the law, you are not a doer of the law but a judge. There is one lawgiver and judge, he who is able to save and to destroy. But who are you that you judge your neighbor?" (Jas. 4:11-12)

The catechism of the Book of Common Prayer asks: "What is the Church?" Answer: "The Church is the community of the New Covenant." You see, it's a community, a *body*, something organic, not at all like a committee, a task force, or a contractual organization. The church is not *organized* religion, although it must organize itself to function in this world where function is supreme.

But as Reinhold Niebuhr once remarked, "All birth in the realm of man's historic institutions is rebirth. The old must die in order that the new self may be born...But the new self, whether in men or in nations, cannot be born if the old self evades the death of repentance, seeking rather to establish itself in its old security and old isolation."

"What is the ministry of the laity?" asks the catechism. Answer: "The ministry of lay persons is to represent Christ and his Church; to bear witness to him wherever they may be; and, according to the gifts given them, to carry on Christ's work of reconciliation in the world...."

That's our rule of life, Virginia. Reconciliation. The catechism calls it a work. But again, I don't think that means that a person goes around "reconciling"—working at being a reconciler. We don't say to ourselves, "Ah, there is a fight going on between Brother Jonas and Sister Abigail. I'll just step in there and reconcile them." No, I think reconciliation is a matter of faithfulness, loyalty, to the body, the community. Faithfulness places us there for others. The reconciliation takes place through us, not by us. It takes place among us. One of the most obnoxious of persons in this world is the one who tries to make a self-work out of reconciliation. Now, please remember this: what we are talking about applies only to the church, the Body of Christ. We can't—shouldn't—force this standard of non-judging and reconciliation on the rest of the world. The world doesn't recognize either the judgment of God, or the reconciliation. The world lives by self-interest and must be protected from its own competitive savagery. It must live by complaints, accusations, and judgments.

There is the story of Abba Poemen, one of the desert fathers. One day some thieves came into the cave of a hermit who lived in the mountains. The brothers in the neighborhood heard the old man cry out. They ran to his cave, captured the robbers, and took them to the magistrate, who put them in jail. The more the brothers thought about what they had done, the more it bothered them: "We are the cause that these men have been put in prison." So they went to visit Abba Poemen to tell him about it. He wrote to the old man saying, "Two things have happened. Consider the first betrayal of your vocation, then examine the second. If you had not failed in the first instance, the second betrayal would not have occurred." When the old hermit heard the reading of Abba Poemen's letter, he rushed out of his cave, went to the city, got the robbers out of jail, and freed them from public torture.

Now, what's the point? Well, the thieves were not monks. They live by standards that the world teaches them. The world teaches them to get what they can, to win, to succeed. In such a world, peace can be kept only by putting robbers in jail. So in one sense the old hermit had no business running into the city and freeing the thieves. Robbers should be put in jail. The monk's, the hermit's life of non-judgment and reconciliation applies only to the community of the New Covenant, which lives by faithfulness and reconciliation. But there's a hitch to this particular slant on the story. Abba Poemen wrote to the old man saying, "Consider the first betrayal and where it comes from, and then examine the second."

What was he pointing out? Abba Poemen was saying: "Ah, perhaps it is true that robbers break the law and should be put in prison, but is it the responsibility of a monk—one who is faithful to the ministry of reconciliation—to raise such a fuss about the robbers? When you raise a fuss, you are saying, 'Don't harm my property! Don't rob me!' As a monk you have given up property in order to serve others. As a monk you have embarked on a path of finding a self that is not concerned with itself, a self that is not outraged by the needs of others. Men become robbers because they live in a world that lives for its own comfort and possessions. So, when you became so outraged at the thieves, you betrayed your vocation as a monk. Instead you should have taught them by your actions that there is a higher self than the one that makes us into robbers. It was this betrayal of your vocation that brought your brothers in outrage, and led them in outrage over possessions to have robbers put in jail."

I began, Virginia, by saying that I wasn't surprised by people whose behavior is backbiting, who act in hatred and outrage. I find all of those emotions in my own life, every day. And when I decide that someone is a real S.O.B. whom I will never trust again, at times like that I can use my rational sense, my reason, to prove what a bad guy he is, and how justified I am never to trust him again. But that's the reasoning of the ordinary mind, which, of course, is what all rationalism is.

The church is not a community of idealists; it isn't an organization of do-gooders. It isn't an organization of those who can add one cubit to their stature by a list of resolutions. The church, you remember, is the community of the New Covenant. This means it's a community of those who recognize they are haters, gossipers, back-biters, even hypocrites—all unacceptable behavior. We are a community because a new way of living has brought us together. This new way says to us: "Your hypocrisy, your hatred is present not only in your worst moments, but in the best of them. This condition of yours pushes God out of the center of life and onto a cross. However, God accepts what you do to him. He accepts the worst of it, the death that it represents—he accepts that and in doing so, he accepts you and brings new life out of death.

In one of my books I said that religion exists *because* people do bad things. Certainly that's true of Christianity. Christianity isn't idealism; it's realism! It's a realistic awareness of the human condition: no holds barred, no illusions. My Christianity tells me that human beings left to themselves, to go their own way, will create a hell on earth. It tells me why people are haters and hypocrites; and it tells me that even when I understand why, I won't become a paragon of virtue. I belong to a community that gathers regularly to say: *We* have left undone those things that we *ought* to have done; and we have done those things that we ought *not* to have done." That is the principle by means of which the church exists.

You see, it's not merely a case of saying: "Look, God, I've done these bad things this week, but I'll shape up; I'll do better!" That's nonsense! What we confess is our condition, not simply our bad deeds. That's why we say: We are the kind of people—we together—the kind who leave things undone. That's the worst of it—the things undone. That's also why we should say it first, not second, as the Prayer of Confession has it in the revised liturgy. We live for ourselves and leave the good undone. But, of course, there are also those things *done*, like the old hermit who screamed about his property and so demonstrated to people that property is very, very important because it is his. So maybe you ought to get some of your own. So maybe it's okay to be a robber.

You see, Virginia, when people are bothered by the fact that church members don't act like Christians, they usually have the wrong thing in mind. Acting like a Christian is 1) admitting that you hate other people; that you envy them, resent them, covet what they have; admitting that you are so obsessed with doing your own thing that the hungry go hungry, the naked go unclothed, the poor get told they should assert themselves, the prisoner gets holed up to satisfy your desire for revenge, and the earth staggers in vertigo while we smother its breathing space in order to make money and increase possessions. Acting like a Christian is admitting your involvement in all that. Acting like a Christian is 2) judging yourself alone; 3) accepting the grace of God in the eucharist; 4) continuing to live in the body of grace and reconciliation; and 5) being grateful that God doesn't have to depend on your goodness. Any other attitude is not Christian. The people who separate themselves because they think others are not Christian are usually trying to excuse their own behavior. They are clinging to their smug self-esteem, refusing to allow God to break through and reveal to them their true selfhood.

After all, Virginia, who is the Christian? Is she the person who says, "Well, after what I heard about her, and the way I saw her act at that vestry meeting, I frankly don't want to be in the same *room* with her—not even on the same street"? Is she the Christian, or is it the woman with a female disease of twelve years' standing who worms her way through the crowd just to be in the same alley with the Lord of Grace, just to touch the hem of his garment? Which one, Virginia? Is he the person who says, "Well, I've always been an honest man, paid my bills on time, given my customers a fair shake. I'm certainly as good a man as old Harold Nussbaum, senior warden at St. Woebegone's—hey! I know what kind of deals he's been mixed up in"? Is he the Christian, or is it that shyster, that huckster for the local mafia, who sells protection for the little businessman—the man who risks his neck and climbs a tree to be near the Lord of Grace?

Which one is the Christian, Virginia? Is it the pillar of virtue who invites you to his charity ball? "And behold, a woman of the city, who was a sinner, when she learned that *he* was at the party, brought an alabaster flask of ointment, and standing behind him at his feet, weeping, she began to wet his feet with her tears, and wiped them with the hair of her head, and kissed his feet, and anointed them with the ointment." And the man who gave the party said to himself, "If this man were really a Christian, he would know what sort of woman is touching him." Which one is the Christian, the man who gave the ball, or the woman with the cologne?

What do I think all of this means? Well, it's hard to say, but one thing is clear to me, Virginia: the church doesn't seem to understand itself today. I mean, priests and preachers have been hiding something. They've been hiding the truth. And they've been hiding it because the people don't want it revealed. When I was a young man, just out of seminary, I was a lost soul. I had learned very little in college or seminary. What I mean to say is, I had seen no bright lights. I had taken history courses and didn't know what history was. It was all a boring recitation of past facts—names, dates, causes and effects. I've learned since that that isn't history at all. I was serving a church and teaching at a prep school. Then, one day I met a man who taught religion at the college my wife was attending. I had never met a person like him before.

He taught me that people like him were known as glandular types—sweaty, driving, intense, excited, always on the move. But it wasn't that that interested me. He was about ten years my senior, but there was a youthful energy about him. He was a pipe smoker. So was I—those were the days before the winds of righteousness blew the aromatic smoke out of the valley of death. Bruce Morgan was a pipe smoker. The tips of his fingers were always a bit stained from tamping tobacco; his nails always had a black rim of ash soundly tucked away under the edge.

When I listened to him I realized he was talking a different language, but I could tell he knew questions that I'd never asked and he had answers that I wouldn't have had the skills to discover. He was the first real theologian I'd met. He became my teacher. Oh, not in any formal sense.

But I began reading, really reading for the first time in my life. I discovered the issues and how to grapple with them. I discovered the powerful nature of traditional Christian doctrine—there was intellectual excitement. Before that I was an unlearned liberal preacher, passing out trivialities to a long-suffering congregation—often quite successfully. Bruce guided me, often in ways unaware. I learned the profundity of Christian theology and I discovered a word that the church did not want to hear. I remember one day, sitting in Bruce's living room. We were talking about some of the things I've already mentioned in this letter. Bruce re-lit his pipe, pulling deeply on the smoldering embers of a barrel of Rum and Maple. He took a sip of his scotch and said to me, "Well, hell, Richard! The truth of the matter is I find more honest Christian community at the local garage where I get my car fixed than I do in the church."

I nodded and wanted to interrupt with some words of agreement. But Bruce went on: "The trouble is, it's the church that has given me the insight to know that!" I remember that conversation now because St. Anne's and St. Woebegone's need to be reminded of it. We have to break through the phony piety and moralistic pretense. We don't have the right to expect that of priests; and the priests have no right to accept that nonsense and go on sanctifying it. We have got to discover the honest community of gutsy humanity that the church really represents—a family of those whom Martin Luther called *simul justus, simul peccator*, simultaneously saints and sinners.

J.D. Salinger's novel *Franny and Zooey* is the story of a young woman who has discovered the terror that lies at the heart of existence. She's discovered the fragility of existence and she's sick, literally sick. Some would say it was a nervous breakdown. Not so, rather a necessary stage on the pilgrimage of anyone who honestly struggles with the meaning of life, the truth of it. Her brother Zooey is a blatant realist. He knows all about philosophical, religious, and theological issues. He and his mother are talking about Franny's problem, and about her boyfriend, a guy named Lane. Zooey thinks Lane is a phony. Zooey is shaving while this conversation goes on. He's just told his mother that Lane is "a charm boy and a fake"—a young man with an ulterior motive for everything he does. His mother says, "Oh, it's impossible to talk to you! But absolutely impossible. I don't know why I try, even. You're just like Buddy. You think everybody does something for some *peculiar reason*. You don't think anybody calls anybody else up without having some nasty, selfish *reason* for it."

"Exactly," says Zooey, "in nine cases out of ten. And this Lane pill isn't the exception, you can be sure. Listen, I talked with him for twenty deadly goddamn minutes one night while Franny was getting ready to go out, and I say he's a big nothing." [Zooey] reflected, holding the stroke of his razor. "What in hell was it he was telling me? Something very *winning*. What was it?...Oh, yes. *Yes*. He was telling me he used to listen to Franny and me every week when he was a kid—and you know what he was doing, the little bastard? He was building *me* up at Franny's expense. For absolutely *no reason* except to ingratiate himself and show off his hot little Ivy League intellect." Zooey put out his tongue and gave a subdued, modified Bronx cheer. "Phooey," he said, and resumed using his razor. "Phooey, I say, on all white-shoe college boys who edit their campus literary magazines. Give me an honest con man any day."[†]

Shall I paraphrase Zooey, Virginia? Do I have to? The church often plays at being "white-shoe college boys who edit their campus literary magazines." We aren't honest! We pretend that being a Christian is being a white-shoe college boy—a phony. But, near as I can tell, being a Christian is being an *honest* con man instead of a dishonest one.

Back in the late fifties, when rock 'n roll hit the scene, Eldridge Cleaver used to say that rock 'n roll was white man finding his soul. It was Pat Boone getting those white shoes all scuffed up. It was movin' with blue suede shoes. It was being a human being. It was like Jack Lemmon in that movie with Shirley MacLaine, "The Apartment." Jack's been giving out the key to his apartment so his boss can use it to rendezvous with Shirley. And all along the boss is dishonest with her, pretending to be Mr. Upright—that he will one day marry her. Jack gets angry and shouts at the boss, "Be a Mensch." Be a human being! Jesus Christ is the key to being a mensch, an honest person! He's the end of white-shoe college boys.

[†] J. D. Salinger, *Franny and Zooey* (New York: Bantam Books, 1972), p. 98.

So tell your friends, Virginia! Tell the vestry! Tell the priests, if you have to. Tell them, Be a mensch! Be an *honest* con, and you may discover that you are less a con than you thought—or than you once were.

Yours in Christ

"When Christianity Doesn't Make Sense"

Dear Mr. Potter,

I know we have met only briefly. It was over cocktails at the home of Jim and Lesley Oldham. I had forgotten our conversation until just recently, when a comment of yours returned like an echo from some deep canyon of time. Anyhow, I overheard some students talking in the hallway after a class in World Religions. "You know," said one, "what really surprises me is that all this stuff is man-made. I mean, all these religions—just a lot of people's attempts to create something they think they need. But do they really need it? Or, anyhow, none of it's really true, is it?"

I listened. I thought, Hey! That young man has made a profound discovery, only he probably doesn't know how profound it really is. And maybe no one will ever show him. Just then your comment came to mind. I could hear it, as if it had been uttered only a moment before. At the Oldham party I heard you say, "Well! I'm a man who deals every day with cold, hard facts in a cold, harsh world. I told my wife—I said to her, 'Dear, I'll go back to St. Woebegone's with you if you could just show me it's not all just wishful thinking. To me, Christianity just makes no rational sense!'"

When I recalled your words, I wanted to laugh. I'm sorry for that, because I don't want to take your thoughts lightly. But I was just thinking: what would happen to our world if people only did things that made rational sense? Or, more precisely, there are many things that make rational sense to some people that make no sense to me. A lot of things that make sense to some people are destructive, evil if you will. It makes perfectly rational sense to terrorists that they should hold innocent hostages in some hole-in-the-wall in Beirut. Apartheid in South Africa is very rational to the government. Hitler's moves to make way for the prosperity of the Third Reich made rational sense; and Communism is about as rational a political and economic scheme as it's possible to have—given the idealistic goal of a classless society.

Forgive me for bringing up the words of a poet. But I like what T. S. Eliot says in "Choruses from 'The Rock'." The words always make me laugh; and few other people see the humor. Eliot puts it this way: "Where there is no temple there shall be no homes." Not funny so far, right?

> Though you have shelters and institutions,
> Precarious lodgings while the rent is paid,
> Subsiding basements where the rat breeds
> Or sanitary dwellings with numbered doors
> Or a house a little better than your
>   neighbor's...

Now I think it starts getting a little funny here. I mean, picture it: we ignore the temple, he says. The result: there are no real homes, just the constant investment of mortgage and rent to keep a roof over our heads, shelters that demand more and more of us; shells that are "investments" until we move on to our next level of investment. Not homes, but investment prisons. That's funny—perfectly rational, but funny! It gets even funnier:

> When the Stranger says: "What is the meaning of this
>   city?
> Do you huddle close together because you love each
>   other?"
> What will you answer? "We all dwell
>   together
> To make money from each other"? or "This is a
>   community"?[†]

When I read those very simple lines for the first time, they were a revelation. A vision. I pictured this very busy world. So busy. People working with charts and calculators. People producing

---

[†] T. S. Eliot, *The Complete Poems and Plays, 1909-1950* (New York: Harcourt, Brace and World, 1952), p. 103.

copy after copy of reports and sales prospectus booklets. Having ulcers. Heart attacks. What is the meaning of this network, this frantic busyness? Why, "to make money from each other"! If that isn't a funny picture, I don't know what is. But from the perspective of the participants, it makes rational sense.

I guess I'm writing to you, Mr. Potter, because I want to take your objection to Christianity seriously. I hope you mean what you say. I hope that you're really concerned about the "rational" sense of it, because, you see, I don't think "rational" sense is much of a warrant for doing anything. What I really mean is that you can make sense out of anything that you want to.

Let me try to answer you in another way. I think rationality can be the great illusion. It can lead us to believe that our ordinary minds can actually control the world. When I want something to "make sense," it usually means I want it to conform to my expectations.

Let me tell you a story. It's about the Buddha, Sakyamuni Buddha. Strange that I should use a story about the Buddha to clear up a point about Christianity. But I don't believe that's out of place at all, because I've learned so much about my Christianity as a result of my encounter with Buddhism.

Anyhow, this is a story about one of the master's disciples who visited him one day and spoke to him in this way: "O Blessed One, I have been in meditation, and these are the thoughts that have come to me. I thought: the Blessed One has left many things unexplained, without rational explanation. In fact, he has ignored them. He has not answered the question of whether the world is eternal, or not eternal; he has not told us how it is that the saint neither exists nor does *not* exist after death. I am bothered by the fact that the Blessed One hasn't explained these things. Now, I have decided that if the Blessed One will explain to me either that the world is eternal, or that it isn't eternal; if he will explain that the saint neither exists nor does not exist after death—if he will explain these things, I shall follow the path of the Blessed One. If the Blessed One will not explain to me that the world is eternal, or that it is not eternal, or that the saint neither exists nor does not exist after death; then, in that case I will abandon the path and return to the life of the every day." And so the disciple went on in his demand that the master provide the " rational" sense he was seeking.

" Tell me, my friend," asked the sage of the Sakya, " Did I ever say to you, 'Come, follow me on the path, lead the religious life with me and I will explain to you either that the world is eternal or that it is not eternal...or that the saint neither exists nor does not exist after death'?"

" No! Certainly not, Reverend Sir."

" Or did you ever say to me, 'I will follow the path with the Blessed One on condition that he explain to me either that the world is eternal or that it is not eternal...or that the saint neither exists nor does not exist after death'?"

" No! Certainly not, Reverend Sir!"

" Then, if that is the case, what is the cause of your anger and why do you approach me in this way? If a person comes to me and says, 'I will not follow the path of the Blessed One until he shall explain to me that the world is eternal, or that the world is not eternal...I will not lead the religious life until the Blessed One explain that the saint neither exists nor does not exist after death'— that person would die before the Enlightened One had ever explained these matters. The entire situation is as if a person had been seriously wounded by an arrow thickly smeared with poison, and his friends and colleagues, his father and mother, his brothers and sisters had procured the services of a physician or a surgeon, and the wounded man were to say, 'I will not permit the arrow to be removed until I have learned whether the person who wounded me belonged to the warrior caste, or to the Brahmin caste, or to the agricultural caste, or to the menial caste.'

" Or, again, as if the wounded man were to say, 'I will not have this arrow removed until I have been told the name of the man who shot it, and to what clan he belongs.'

" Or again, if he were to say, 'I will not permit the arrow to be taken out until I have learned whether the person who wounded me was tall, or short, or of middle height.'

" Or again, if he were to say, 'I will not have this arrow removed until I have found out whether the one who shot it was black, or swarthy, or yellow of skin.' You see, my friend, such a person would die before he could learn what he demands to know. The truth of the path does not depend upon a dogma that the world is eternal; it does not depend upon a teaching that the world is *not* eternal. Whether it is true that the world is eternal or that the world is not eternal, there still remain birth, old age, death, sorrow, mourning, misery, grief, and despair. It is these matters that the path extinguishes.

"So remember, my son, what it is that I have explained and what I have not explained. I have not explained that the world is eternal; I have not explained that the world is not eternal; I have not explained that the world is finite; I have not explained that the world is infinite; I have not explained that the soul and body are one and the same; I have not explained that the soul is one thing and the body another; I have not explained that the saint exists after death; I have not explained that the saint does not exist after death; I have not explained that the saint both exists and does not exist after death; I have not explained that the saint neither exists nor does not exist after death.

"And why, my son? Why have I not explained this? Because, my son, this profits not, nor has it to do with the path of the Blessed One. When a person thinks he has found an explanation for such matters, it is like learning the color of the skin of the one who shot the arrow, while the poison eats away at his life. These matters do nothing to bring the wisdom that is necessary to the life of compassion and enlightenment, the end of suffering. These matters do not profit; they do not lead to edification. That is why I have not explained them.

"What have I explained? Suffering, have I explained; the origin of suffering have I explained; the cessation of suffering have I explained; and the path of leading to the cessation of suffering have I explained. Why have I explained this? Because, my son, this *does* profit; this *does* lead to edification. Always bear in mind what it is that I have explained; and what it is that I have not explained."[†]

Well, there you have it, Mr. Potter. I don't know what you think of that story. I think it is one of the most profound stories I've ever encountered. And why do I blacken these pages with the account of it? I hope you know the answer to that, at least partly. The first thing it tells me is that the person who demands "rational" sense of the Christian Path before he will follow it—well, he makes his demands because he wants the world to meet the specifications of his own self-centered ego.

The story also tells me that the truth of the redemption that is represented by Jesus Christ does not depend upon satisfactory answers to metaphysical and philosophical speculation. It depends upon following the Path. It's that simple. Remember, the Gospel accounts do not tell us that Jesus went about conducting inquirers' classes. He did not say, "Let me answer your questions about whether there is a God or not. Let me explain to you why Hurricane Gilbert takes innocent lives." He did not say, "Let me explain to you why some evil folks live in mansions while the good people are homeless." He did not say these things! He did not say, "Now, that I've answered your questions, tell me, how many of you are ready to join my movement?" He *did* say, "Come, follow me!" and they left their nets and

---

[†] Adapted from E. A. Burtt, ed., *The Teachings of the Compassionate Buddha* (New York: New American Library, 1955), pp. 32-36.

their carpenters' benches. He did say, "Come unto me, all you who know your misery and your helplessness and your stress."

You see, Mr. Potter, there's a very important principle at work here. It says that the credibility of the rational mind depends upon the commitments we have made. The rational mind can serve many masters. This principle says, you will understand the matters of God and of evil and misery, things finite and infinite, things practical and impractical—you will understand these matters in the course of traveling the path that is the Way, the Truth, and the Life. Before that, you will never understand; and the poison will go deeper into your system while you wait for your kind of rationality. When you discover the suffering that goes on in the Heart of the Universe, then you will understand suffering, and you will share in God's compassion for the world. You see, Mr. Potter, you can't define God and then go looking for your definition. You must meet God on the path; otherwise all you will ever meet are your own shadows.

Let me take another approach to this business of the rational mind. The rational mind is made to do two things. It is made to examine and measure, and tinker with the things of this world, most of which are the product of that tinkering mind in the first place. But the mind is also made to recognize that its ways of thinking about the things of this world cannot be used to deal with the business of the ultimate order and meaning of existence. The mind that talks about a straight line as the shortest distance between two points is not the mind that can talk about God or salvation—such matters as that. I know. I know. You're asking: well, how many minds do we have? Believe me, I'm not going to get mixed up in some discussion of the physiology of the brain—something like that. No! But it's clear to me, from the study of religion, that the mind does operate on at least two levels, in two ways. The mind knows logic; it knows how to deduce and how to induce. But the mind also knows that it's in love. The mind also knows that tomorrow may be a better day. The mind knows how to imagine.

The mind can imagine. What does that mean? It means that the mind can respond directly to whatever meaning and order it encounters in the universe. The mind can receive images that it will then use logic, deduction, induction—it will use rationality, reason—to clarify. In other words, the mind takes the images it receives and tests them, tries them, puts them to work, to create. A rational mind that is not able to receive images will soon be an enslaved mind. What else did the prophet mean when he said: "Where there is no vision the people perish!" That observation is literally valid. Imagination is the mark and the measure of freedom. It provides the substance and the inspiration for the use of whatever "rational sense" any of us has, Mr. Potter.

Now, most of the time we spend ignoring the power of the imagination to receive images. And unless the imagination can receive the image of God, people will remain slaves to their senses. They close their minds to the imagination because the imagination isn't easy to control. The rational mind is easy to control. Remember, it will do your bidding, but in the end you will be imprisoned inside a cocoon of your own creation— which is a metaphor of hell without the fire. A much more dangerous one, inasmuch as fire usually backs us off from it.

I recall a poem of old Robert Frost's. Remember him? He offered a poem at John Kennedy's inauguration. Frost was a craggy old soul. He saw behind the ordinary. He could look at a pasture, two tramps in mud time, the death of the hired man, a mending wall—look at such ordinary things and see much more than most of us see. Why? Because his mind developed the power of the imagination to receive images; and his rational sense took those images and communicated truth that we need to know and often ignore. He who has ears to hear, let him hear. He who has eyes to see, let him see. Well, all people have eyes and ears, right? Or, do they?

Frost wrote a poem called "The Cocoon." In it he observes a haze over the meadow in the evening air and ponders its source. Is it the smoke from "one poor house alone"? No one has ventured from the place in all the time he has been watching.

> The inmates may be lonely womenfolk.
> I want to tell them that with all this smoke
> They prudently are spinning their own cocoon
> and anchoring it to an earth and moon
> From which no winter gale can hope to blow it—
> Spinning their own cocoon did they but know it.[†]

I don't think I need comment on that, do I? A cocoon of your own creation—a mind with ration-

[†] Edward Connery Lathem, ed., *The Poetry of Robert Frost* (New York: Holt, Rinehart and Winston, 1979), p. 248.

ality deprived of imagination, closed in upon itself, without freedom.

I think Christianity is saying that Jesus Christ is the restorer of human imagination. He helps us out of the cocoon, makes it possible for the mind to receive the image of God, shows us our own Christ-nature. The ordinary mind cannot see such things. It has nothing to go on. It's been robbed of deep imagination. The ordinary mind, a very *rational* mind, is like the fish who was greeted one day by his friend the tortoise. "Good day, my friend," said the tortoise, "I have just come back from a walk on the land." "Of course," said the fish, "you mean you were swimming." The tortoise tried to explain that it was impossible to swim on the land, that it was firm, that one could only walk on something so solid. But the fish insisted there could be nothing like that, that it had to be liquid like the sea, with waves, and that one had to be able to dive and swim there.

The ordinary mind is like the fish. That's why Jesus does not just talk about your Christ-nature. He doesn't just talk about restoring the human imagination so that it may receive the image of God. Talk might appeal to the ordinary mind. But it wouldn't restore anything. It wouldn't make the fish understand what the tortoise was saying. No, Jesus is crucified! He accepts the results of the thinking of the rational people of the ordinary mind. And in doing so, he reveals the fact that God is something other than what we expect him to be. God is not a monarch! A dictator! God is Father-Mother! God is the Heart of Compassion that holds all things together even when all things reject him. No ordinary mind can understand that! Only a mind whose imagination has been stirred to follow the Path.

You know, it's too bad that the Christian pulpit (and Christian lay people with their use of the Bible, for that matter)—it's too bad that we have declawed the parables of Jesus, made them into "moral tales." Actually, many of those parables were originally told to shock people. To shock them out of relying on their ordinary minds, their ordinary ways of thinking. You see, the truth behind every great religious tradition is a truth that only a transformed mind can understand—a mind that has been shocked out of its ordinariness. Zen Buddhism and the Sufi tradition of the Islamic world are filled with tales about minds that are transformed. The Zen master forces curious statements called *koans* upon his disciples. He tries to frustrate them, to show them the limitations of the ordinary mind. And when the frustration is greatest, that is the moment when new mind breaks through.

New mind is imagination, the power to receive an image that no ordinary mind can conceive. We call it the image of God. What else do you suppose the Gospel means when it says, "He who would save his life shall lose it, but whoever loses his life for my sake (for the sake of the Christ who is the image of God) shall save it." At the moment when we discover the ineffectiveness and virtual non-existence of this demanding self to which we are attached—at that moment an image of a mind compassionate for all things is born.

Once Zen Master Kyong Ho was traveling with his student Zen Master Mang Gong. Mang Gong's leg began to hurt so much that he finally had to sit down under a tree. He found he couldn't get up again. This was a big problem because they had to be at a certain temple before nightfall, and there were still many miles to go. So Kyong Ho left Mang Gong under the tree and walked away. Soon he came to a field where some peasants were working. One of them was a girl of sixteen or seventeen. Kyong Ho went up to her, took her in his arms and gave her a passionate kiss. The girl's parents and the other peasants were horrified, particularly when they realized Kyong Ho was a monk. They were outraged and began to chase Kyong Ho across the fields. Kyong Ho headed straight for the tree, shouting, 'Get up! Run for your life!' When Mang Gong saw him coming closer with the mob of angry peasants behind him, he leaped up and ran away at full speed. They reached the temple before nightfall. That's what it takes to break through the controls of the ordinary mind.

How is it possible? How can I assume that a mere epistle could possibly address the issue you raised that day, Mr. Potter? There are so many more things to say. "Christianity makes no rational sense," you said. I assure you, the matter is very complex! Yet at the same time it's very simple—as simple as being hit on the head with an apple while you doze under a tree. One thing is certain; there are ways to meet the challenge you present. The question is: Are you serious enough to pursue the matter? I have learned long ago that it is impossible to learn until you are willing to be taught.

Indulge me one final observation. I am skeptical about a person or a civilization that tries to build a world upon the foundation of its own immediate rational sense. What we build is hell on earth, either in terms of utter chaos and terror, or in the illusory way of Robert Frost's cocoon. Much of what we please to do in our own rational manner is ugly, low-down and disgusting—partly because even when we mean to do something decent, we are too myopic, too weak-willed, too addle-pated to bring it to pass. Humanity must be redeemed of its ordinary "rational" sense.

I saw a headline in the paper this past week: "Arizona State University Scholar Hot on the Trail of Artificial Intelligence." My first thought was: "Why not? We haven't done so well with the real thing." My second thought was: "Artificial Intelligence? I thought that's what we've been using all along."

I want to end this letter with a portion of a kind of verse drama by Robert Frost. It was called "A Masque of Mercy", and the setting is a bookstore late at night. It's closing time. The characters are the keeper, his wife, a man named Paul, one named Jesse Bel, and a fugitive by the name of Jonah. At one point they were talking about revolutionaries. Paul reminds his hearers that Christ was not the cause of the world's violence, as some have charged. The Nazarene did not really cross "old Attic grace and Spartan discipline with violence." Violence has been a commonplace in the world, says Paul. Christianity did not bring it.

> Christ came to introduce a break with logic
> That made all other outrage seem as child's play:
> The Mercy on the Sin against the Sermon.
> Strange no one ever thought of it before Him...

The keeper replies:

> Paul's constant theme. The Sermon on the Mount
> Is just a frame-up to insure the failure
> Of all of us, so all of us will be
> Thrown prostrate at the Mercy Seal for Mercy.[†]

True. That *is* Paul's constant theme. And it remains an insight at the heart of Christianity. Christ is a break with logic that gives our ordinary rationality a new direction. Christ is the beginning of wisdom. His presence is a recognition of the inadequacy of ordinary rationality to deal with ultimate concerns.

Yours in Christ

[†] *Ibid.*, p. 511.

"When You No Longer Know What Faith Means"

Dear Clifford,

Your letter reached me while I was on vacation. I had some time of solitude and silence to think about it. Then just this week I received some notes from people after a class. One of them said: "Among my thinking friends the greatest spiritual problem appears to be lack of faith in a personal God...my greatest spiritual problem is knowing when to let go of a problem and to trust God to solve it; when to 'let go and let God.'" I won't tell you who wrote that letter, but I think it's a bit dishonest. When people tell me they aren't able to "let go and let God," they aren't really expressing their own thoughts and feelings. They are using a phrase they read in some "How To" book or heard some phrase-making television preacher deliver.

You see, it's not at all clear to me that "let go and let God" sums up the Gospel. I'm also not sure that God is a solver of problems. Human beings have become problem-solvers—they think everything is a problem that should be defined and then solved. And so they think God should follow suit. It should be pretty clear that problem-solving seldom gets to the heart of the matter. Take, for instance, modern applied science—technology, if you want to call it that. Technology is the problem-solving mind, par excellence. We see a disease. So we say, let's try to find out what the problem is, then let's find a solution. A committee is appointed or a research team is set up: define the problem and solve it. Okay? A solution is found. Two years later we discover that the solution has caused another problem.

Now, what's wrong with that? Well, isn't it rather obvious that life isn't reducible to a problem? Of course, we have to do this kind of work. We have to try to solve problems. We have little choice. We go on defining problems and solving them, creating new ones, defining them, and solving them. That's okay! We should accept that. But instead we assume that we are addressing the central issue of the meaning of life by solving a problem; and that's nonsense. We assume we are not only merely solving a problem we ourselves have created and defined, but that we are putting an end to human misery. We—by our problem-solving! We assume with Paul Harvey that every day things are getting better and better. The Republican party at Evensong!

But it isn't true and that's why we are so disappointed in God. He doesn't play our game! He doesn't solve the problems we define for him! Instead, he is the constant reminder that only by transcending our stubborn view of life-as-a-problem will we find the truth, and the peace—do you remember what peace it is? The paradox of peace—that passes all understanding! " My peace I give unto you! Not as the world [the problem-solving, information-understanding world] giveth give I to you."

So Clifford, old friend, when the writer of that letter said that the greatest spiritual problem of his friends is lack of faith in a personal God, he revealed his hand. He was saying, my friends have a problem—they lack faith in a personal God! They say they just can't accept the fact that such a God exists. They agree that there may be some kind of force—you know, 'May the force be with you.' It seems to be admissible to say things like that. But a personal God that is involved in existence? That's too much! So, my friends have this problem, says the letter-writer. Let's get to solving it for them. Do you see the issue? A person is never a problem! God is never a problem! If you define faith in a personal God as a problem, then all you will come up with is an answer that solves problems, but not a relationship to a personal being. Faith then becomes some kind of tinkering, fix-it-up action, to solve the problem. But I think faith is something else entirely. Faith is not a work, not a tinkering, mechanical activity meant to solve a problem. Faith isn't a solution or a resolution. It's not an act of ruling out the incredible, a blind commitment. It's something else!

But before I get too deeply into this business, I want to get back to your letter.

"I decided [you wrote] that I'd better write to you today (Sunday), because from Monday through Saturday I'm too busy making a living to deal with esoteric spiritual problems. You see, I have a harder and harder time, trying to integrate my spiritual convictions and loving, peaceful state of mind into my daily life. I'm at the point where I tell myself I need a strong abiding faith in God, but I no longer know how to get it. I no longer know what faith means.

"In addition, someone who is single like me has to deal with the need for sex, love and companionship. I saw a bumper sticker last week that said, "The Only Friend You Need is Jesus." I would like to think that's true, but people have needs that simply can't be transcended in modern society. At the very least, we all need someone to respond to us, in a human way. So faith—what is faith anyhow in the midst of all this? And who has time for it except for a little glow on a Sunday morning?"

Now, Clifford, that's a tough letter. But it's an honest one. Of course, I'm a little surprised at it. You always seemed to me to be a person who had everything well in place. Of course, I think you are trying to find something you call "faith." It's almost as if there's something "out there" that you want and don't have. You tell me that you're all busied up in this hectic society, trying to coax out a living—six days a week because that's what the business expects of you. "I'm too busy making a living to deal with esoteric spiritual problems." Esoteric? Who says faith is esoteric? *You* do! Because you want it to be. You want it to be something "out there" you don't really have time for—what with making a living, finding love, companionship, sexual fulfillment. You want that little Sunday morning glow to be a big glow that it would be nice to have, only you don't really think it has anything to do with sex, love, friendship, and making a living.

There's the story of Nasrudin, the Sufi teacher. He used to take his donkey across the border every day, with its wicker baskets laid with straw. When he got home at night he admitted to being a smuggler and the word got out. So the border guards began searching him. Every time he made the trip they searched. They frisked his body, sifted the straw, soaked the straw in water, sometimes burned it. They found nothing. But Nasrudin was looking more and more like a prosperous merchant. He retired and went to live in another land. Years later one of the customs officers met him there.

"Ah, you can tell me now without fear of arrest; what was it you were smuggling in those days when we searched you to no avail?"

"Donkeys," said Nasrudin.

You see, Clifford, the customs officials didn't see the obvious. They were looking for something out there somewhere, something special, something sinister or mysterious. They missed what was right before their eyes. Faith is having eyes to see the donkeys, Clifford. They're right there. Faith isn't some esoteric business. It's an everyday *seeing* and it has to do with making a living, sex, love, and companionship. If you "find" it, that's where it'll be.

There's a little passage in the early pages of Edward Abbey's *Desert Solitaire* that rings so true for me. It's early dawn, before sunrise, in the canyon lands, the "slickrock desert" outside of Moab, Utah. Abbey is sitting alone in the doorway of his housetrailer, with a mug of steaming coffee just as the flaming orb of the sun comes up. "I am not alone after all," he writes. "Three ravens are wheeling near the balanced rock, squawking at each other and at the dawn. I'm sure they're as delighted by the return of the sun as I am and I wish I knew their language. I'd sooner exchange ideas with the birds on earth than learn to carry on intergalactic communications with some obscure race of humanoids on a satellite planet from the world of Betelgeuse. First things first. The ravens cry out in husky voices, blue-black wings flapping against the golden sky. Over my shoulder comes the sizzle and smell of frying bacon. That's the way it was this morning."[†]

That's the way it *is*, friend Clifford. Everything is so close, waiting. Waiting to be seen, to be smelled, touched, and kissed. Waiting for the eyes and ears of faith to see what is up close, in touch with your fingers. Esoteric? My God, no, Clifford! Watch for the donkeys!

The other morning I was taking my morning run. My dog Fritzi runs with me. She usually moves out ahead of me a half block or so. It's part of her destiny to check the passing lawns for the

---

[†] Edward Abbey, *Desert Solitaire* (New York: Ballantine Books, 1968), p. 7.

scent of previous canine travelers. It was cooler than usual, the sun pressing its claims against the red tile of the roofs of Santo Tomas, leaving the tall stems and fronds of palm trees in mood indigo. I run with my eyes directed to the roadway twenty feet ahead, often thinking about a lecture or plotting the day's assignments, the subtle sounds of "Kyrie Eleison, Christe Eleison, Kyrie Eleison" cooking away deep within me. Usually I'm very conscious of the way ahead. I don't enjoy the running, but it's a "habit of the heart"—fifteen years of doing what I must do, like brushing my teeth. Suddenly I realized I was ready to cross the street directly across from my driveway. Impossible! I thought! I had no memory, no awareness whatsoever of the last quarter mile or so. It was an uncanny sensation—as if my body had been merged with the world around me, my legs moving in rhythm with the pulse of the universe, at one with a kind of nothingness that isn't "nothing" as I imagine it to be. I had been conscious, but not *self*-conscious. A vessel ready to "catch grace as a man fills his cup under a waterfall," as Annie Dillard puts it. Faith is catching grace under a waterfall!

Catch it if you can! I have a little cottage, a modest place with tilting floors, one bedroom, on a country lane a mile or two north of the center of the little town of Payson, Arizona. Grey, with white trim, pressed in tightly by several huge oak trees that threaten the little place in a bad storm. I don't get to visit my little cottage very often, but when I'm there and the weather permits, I sit on the front porch on my white rocking chair. I learned rocking chair sitting when I was a little boy. It was one of the greatest things my parents taught me. Rocking chair sitting is rhythm sitting—it's "just sitting." Like those Israelis and other Orthodox Jews from all over the world who stand before the Western Wall in Jerusalem—just rocking back and forth, the words of ancient prayers swaying in harmony with the movement of centuries of suffering, of flight—in rhythm with the Heart of the Universe.

I like to "just sit" on my rocking chair—I like to rhythm sit. I stare across the meadow westward toward the bushy knob of the national forest. The sun becomes a blazing orb that suddenly strikes the shaggy grass of the meadow. Before me everything is aflame! But not consumed! The self-consciousness burned out of it, more beautiful than ever. Seen as the eye of God sees it; seen as the Christ-nature in all things—like donkeys walking, like cups filling with spring water.

I think, Clifford—I think that faith is not so strange as it seems. It is no less significant, no less possible in the time-bomb moments of this century than it was in earlier times. Grace is always occurring before your eyes. Producing faith! Burning away in the ordinary things. Sometimes when you're running, or just-sitting, rhythm sitting, rocking. But I suspect there are also moments at the water-cooler, in front of the computer screen.

The world is so full of evidence of the holy. In its beauty and its ugliness, its good and evil, there is a sense that human existence is so much "more than" we allow it to be. And what we call faith is the special way of *knowing* this "more than" quality. Isn't that what John Donne is saying in this sermon?

"O Eternal and most glorious God, who sometimes in thy justice dost give the dead bodies of the saints to be meat unto the fowls of heaven, and the flesh of thy saints unto the beasts of the earth, so that their blood is shed like water, and there is none to bury them; who sometimes sell'st thy people for naught, and dost not increase thy wealth by their price, and yet never leav'st us without the knowledge that precious in thy sight is the death of thy saints, enable us, in life and death, seriously to consider the value, the price of a soul. It is precious, O Lord, because thine image is stamped and printed upon it; precious because the blood of thy Son was paid for it; precious because thy blessed Spirit, the Holy Ghost, works upon it and tries it by His diverse fires; and precious because it is entered into thy revenue and made a part of thy treasure."[†]

Precious and close. The fires are right before your eyes!

Perhaps I've tried your patience, my friend. For these moments, in this particular letter, there was no way for me to do otherwise than what I've done. I've said these things because the words have chosen me to give them utterance. It was the way in these moments to try to confront you with the awesome reality of faith, its day-by-day presence to the eye that sees.

[†] *The Sermons of John Donne*, Evelyn M. Simpson and George R. Potter, eds., vol. 8 (Berkeley, CA: University of California Press, 1956), p. 61.

If you discover the truth, then you will be ready to ask questions. You see, until you learn this, you will be too attached to your questions. And you will expect too much of the answers. So you will never really understand what faith means. For instance, the problem of doubt. Often a person wonders, why is it that I am always doubting things? Why can't I have a firm faith in a personal God? Sometimes I doubt there is such a thing. I can believe in a kind of force or energy, some kind of a "supreme being," I suppose. But a personal God—now, that's something else. You see? You see? The doubt is always with me. Why can't I have enough faith to overcome it?

Now, if that's what's troubling you, what can we say? Do you remember my mentioning the other letter I received—the note, from the student after a class? The note wanted to find a way to "let go and let God." I wonder what would happen if we said, "Let God go and let yourself go"?

Now, before you report me to the bishop on a charge of heresy, hear me out. When you worry about doubt, isn't it because you're attached to a notion of God that you think you should have? Your self-consciousness has latched on to something called "God" that you hope will satisfy you. So any hint that this God may not exist or that he may not be what you want, sets you to fretting, to worrying. Doubt sets in! Doubt is another form of self-conscious desire. You doubt because you are secretly pleased that you have such mighty powers. You are attached to the God of your self-consciousness. You doubt this God of your self-consciousness. So you are really attached to your self-consciousness. Ah, but you are more than that—more than self-consciousness and its God.

Let God go! Don't worry about God. God can take care of himself. And if you let him go, you can let yourself go. And if you let such things go, it will be because faith has made it possible. If you let God go, he returns on his own terms, right in the midst of things, which is the only way you can know him anyhow. Then you are free! God frees you to be *you*, not to be what you want. Then you can doubt. When you doubt, doubt! Don't worry about it. Just doubt!

And so you will discover that doubt is really the underside of faith. Doubt strengthens faith. When I doubt, I'm dissatisfied with what I've been thinking or believing. I'm disappointed in what someone has told me is true. I'm questioning my view of the ordinary! And, you see, often our understanding of God is very ordinary. Doubt can be understood as the gracious movement of God, telling us to "let God go"—let God be God, not the object of your designing hopes. Doubt is God saying—let God go, let yourself go—you are a person; therefore you are more than you *think*, and so am I. Come up higher! Doubt is grace, crashing through your desire and attachments, hoping that you will fill your cup under the waterfall, hoping that you will be surprised by faith. Faith is grace received. Faith is the gracious acceptance of doubt. Don't worry about doubt!

What I hope you will begin to see, Clifford, is that faith is not an act of the will. It is not deciding to believe! It isn't believing at all—at least not in the sense of some leap of intellect. Faith is faithfulness, a kind of *knowing* faithfulness. Trust! It's like when you love someone, you're willing to go along. You just *know* you must! You *know* you should! For no particular reason. You let go of yourself for the other. Broken relationships are always the result of attachment to individual desire.

We want the other person to be something, to behave in a certain way—to be sexy, to be responsible as *we* see responsibility. Pretty soon we're so attached to the desire that we can't be faithful to the relationship. We are no longer able to be *for* the other. Faithfulness is going along with life because you know that others are always the measure of your own existence. Remember the great patriarch of Israel. Remember Abraham! He went out not knowing where he was going. He was being faithful to the call of the Holy One, the Other who says, "Let God go! Let yourself go! Follow Me!"

In the eucharistic liturgy, the celebrant says, "Let us give thanks unto the Lord." The people respond: "It is meet and right so to do." That is a statement of faith! Because the congregation is being faithful, it is saying, "This is the only thing we can do!" It says to us that faith isn't the end result of some kind of intellectual search; it isn't even Pascal's "wager." It isn't a solution to a problem, not even the problem of life. "It is meet and right so to do"—that's like saying, Hey! Life is not by my specification! It's much greater, fuller, more joyful than my own personal fantasy. "It is meet and right to be thankful." Gratitude! Faithfulness to the God who gives himself to us.

There is the story of the father of modern Jewish Hasidism, the Baal Shem Tov—Master of the Great Name. He knew his hour was approaching. But a master must always be faithful—in this life, in death, in the life to come. If faithfulness doesn't include those who have gone before us, it isn't worth much. It hasn't really begun to understand God's world. So the Baal Shem Tov promised his disciples that when he arrived in heaven, he would use all his influence to hasten the coming of the Messiah, and when his soul reached heaven, he requested audience with the Redeemer. His wish was granted. It is impossible to refuse the request of a Baal Shem. But he was lifted to such heights of joy, such ecstasy in the presence of the Redeemer, that he forgot his promise.

Well, the Maggid of Mezeritch, successor to the Baal Shem—the Maggid knew of the mishap, and he decided he wasn't about to make the same mistake. "I shall avoid such exaltation," he said. "I shall make no request to see the Messiah. I shall confer with others instead, and so the Redeemer will go down to earth." Ah, but he was disarmed, made into an angel, so that he also forgot what he had promised the people.

Along came Levi-Yitzhak of Berditchev. "I shall be faithful to you," he promised. "The temptations of paradise will not lead me astray. In fact, I shall refuse to enter paradise. I shall say to our Lord, 'Master of the Universe, it is impossible for me to set aside my human responsibilities for heavenly ones. I remind you of what you already know. It is your duty to your children to redeem them. Send them the Messiah. They know they need him. They are not so stubborn as you.'"

Well, Levi-Yitzhak stirred up a hornet's nest. He kept annoying the Master of the Universe, and to their astonishment, the angels had to use force to push him into paradise.

"Don't worry," said Israel of Rizhin, the tzaddik who told this story. "Don't worry! I promise you. I shall resist better and longer than the rest of them. I shall not forget. I shall be faithful!"†

Well, you see, Clifford, that's faith. It's hanging in there. It's resolving to keep faithful even though earth remains a very shaky place to live, even though the Messiah doesn't come, even though you can't force the hand of God. When you discover the truth that life is more than you can make of it, it's the result of revelation, the initiative of the personal God who divests you of your *self*-consciousness, to show you that true person, your true selfhood is bound up with the universe around you. That discovery is the graceful gift of faith. The human being doesn't exist without faith. Without faith our reason flounders. Reason goes this way and that, seeking orientation. Faith ties reason together with imagination and makes us whole beings.

Read the Daily Office, Clifford. You have time. Keep reading it even if it seems to be a chore, even if you get no particular inspiration. Keep doing it. Be faithful! In so doing, you are making it possible for your life to be surprised by visitations of grace! There are some things you just have to do in order to keep your dignity. You have to be a disciple in order to be ready for the truth. And being a disciple is making a promise and sticking by it. Being a disciple is being obedient to something greater than your self-con-

---

† Adapted from Elie Wiesel, *Souls on Fire* (London: Weidenfeld and Nicholson, 1972), pp. 140-141.

sciousness. Being a disciple is accepting a discipline.

Bankei was a Zen master who was very popular. His talks were attended by persons of all rank, by members of many different sects. He never quoted sutras or the works of scholars. He spoke directly from his heart to the hearts of his listeners.

Bankei was so popular that it angered a Nichiren priest because the adherents of his sect went to hear Bankei's lectures. So he came to the temple determined to get into an argument with Bankei. "Hey, Zen teacher!" he shouted. "Wait a minute. These people obey you because they respect you. But I don't respect you. Can you make me obey you?"

"Come here beside me and I'll show you," said Bankei. So the priest pushed his way through the crowd and stood before the teacher. Bankei smiled and said, "Come over to my left side." The priest obeyed. "No, that isn't right," said Bankei, "we can talk better if you are on the right side. Step over here." And so the priest proudly stepped over to the right. "You see," observed Bankei, "you are obeying me and I think you are a very gentle person. Now sit down and listen."

That's it, Clifford. Sit down and listen. Follow the teacher. Do what you must do. That's the only way to be ready for faith—by being faithful. Sit down. Stop making demands. Pray. Listen.

Yours in Christ

"When Your Nephew Joins The Moonies"

My Dear Lydia,

I received your letter only yesterday. George must have forgotten to post it immediately after you wrote it. Perhaps he waited until after your return from the islands—I'm sure it was stuck in his seersuckers.

I'm sorry to learn that you're so despondent. It isn't like you. You wonder, what shall we do about St. Woebegone's? My dear lady, don't be afraid of the welfare of your many generous gifts and bequests. Don't worry, these hallowed walls will be standing long after the Democrats are put to rest.

But you are right to be concerned about the church. Attendance is not what it used to be; and the young people—well, you know—they have ever so much to do. You and I had to be safely tucked in before midnight on a Saturday—at least until we were eighteen. The wild parties were limited to summers at the beach house. But these young folk today—they party any time they feel like it. No one can stop them, all hours of the night. Sunday morning is bound to be hang-over heaven.

Anyhow, they say they don't have the slightest idea of what all this mumbo-jumbo is about. And they don't think we do either. These are trying times for St. Woebegone's. Episcopalians are not so much up and down as they used to be, of course. The new Prayer Book saw to that. I sometimes wonder why the Altar Guild bothered to stitch all those kneelers. The young folks think our liturgy and our vested priests are a far cry from 2 Live Crew.

Pledging is down again this year, they tell me. And some of the people are leaning in the direction of that community church on the next block. I hear it's because they "teach the Bible" there, and they have a witnessing fellowship for each age group. So, you see, Lydia, I understand your depression. But what seems to bother you most is tucked into that final paragraph—not much more than a sentence. I think you're really upset because your nephew joined the Moonies. So I want to spend some time on that subject, if you don't mind, partly because it's probably related to all these other things I just mentioned. If I can write to you about all this, it'll help me to get my own thoughts in order.

First, I think your nephew, Randolph, is a bit of a Johnny-come-lately—sort of last off the mark. I mean, joining the Moonies is not as notorious as it once was. It's no longer a media event, and I don't suppose the movement is growing by leaps and bounds. At least in terms of members. We hear much more about the attractions of New Age religiosity. New Age, of course, is not new at all. Its many forms are all part of the history of religion, and much of what we can say about it goes for the Moonies, too.

Let's face it, one of the reasons for the earlier success (if that's what it was) was that the Moonies, like the Hare Krishnas, the Children of God, and the Divine Light Mission, rode in on the coattails of the 1960s revolution. I'm sure I don't have to remind you, the Sixties were anti-establishment. They opposed everything that *had been*, partly because they felt that the older generations were consummate hypocrites. The sixties generation was a generation of Puritans—for all their sexual pandering, they were Puritans. Because, you see, the Puritans believed that most people gave only lip serve to truth and ideals. As John Winthrop put it: "That which the most maintain as a truth in profession only, we must bring into familiar and constant practice."

I think that latter-day Puritans are much worse than the originals. The originals were not naive about human nature. They didn't think they were perfect. They believed it was up to them to build a holy commonwealth of holy people, but they knew it would be less than the Kingdom of God. Latter-day Puritans are absolute idealists; they believe it's possible to create an ideal world—according to their specifications. That leads to rationalism, which is the assumption that the logic of our ideas must become the prescription for the world's ills. The problem with that notion is that it leads to a very fragmented society in which groups of people with very rational causes are in constant conflict with others. A healthy society is one in which life is held together not by rational contrivance, but by relationships. The world today is filled with many righteous and rational parties, all in a state of agitation.

Most of the Moonies I know are children of the Sixties. They are absolute idealists, and they have discovered that the Unification Church of Sun Myung Moon is an advocate of the kind of world that the rebels of the Sixties represented.

A second thing I must say, Lydia, is that your nephew has obviously been looking for something and no one paid any attention. Let's face it, you and I were raised on a set of beliefs that was greatly at odds with the Christianity we professed. Whether we realized it or not, it made the church seem silly and irrelevant—just something—well, we Pennsylvania Dutch would call it just something you do " for nice."

What do I mean? What are our beliefs? Well, we believe...let's put it this way. We say: "I don't want my son to have to work as hard as I did." We say: "I want my daughter to amount to something." We ask: "What are you studying English literature for, anyway? What kind of a job will that get you? Be a doctor, a lawyer, an engineer, or at least go into business management." Those statements, those questions, represent our creed. They tell what it is we *really* believe in. We often believe in God, or go to church, just to affirm these real beliefs of ours. God is supposed to stamp our passports, be a kind of notary public providing an affidavit for what we want to do. He's supposed to be the power behind the positive thinking we do about our goals, our selfish dreams. If Randolph joins the Moonies, it means that he isn't satisfied with that kind of phony religiousness. He is looking for a path, a way...something that makes a difference, that demands something of him.

Right there you have it, Lydia. Randolph is telling you he's not satisfied with a religion that makes no difference. He knows that true religion means discipline. It means being a disciple. It means that a person is ready to follow, to learn, to grow. Now, don't get me wrong, I'm not saying that the Moonies are right. All I'm saying is that Randolph is looking for something that will make a difference in his life and in the life of the world. He thinks he has found that with the Moonies. Call him a damned fool, if you wish, but—no, Lydia, I take that back—*don't* call him a damned fool. That is one of the first things you must learn. He is *not* a damned fool. Nor are many of those other Moonie associates of his. That I can assure you. I have known many of those people. Those I have known are very intelligent—some of them have taken Ph.D.s from places like Harvard, Yale, Vanderbilt, Claremont, Chicago, Emory, Berkeley. It's true they are often a bit dreamy-eyed, idealistic. Now, I'm no idealist. I'm just the opposite of these folks—if I were an idealist, I wouldn't be a Christian. But I shouldn't discuss that now. The point I have to make is that Moonies are human beings, no less intelligent than the rest of us. They are thinking people. Highly sensitive morally. Give them credit. They have something going for them or they wouldn't have attracted Randolph.

Another thing: we live in the days of consumer religion. This is a consumer age. You and I are primarily consumers. The message that comes through to us every day on the radio, the TV screen, the newspapers and magazines—even through our educational systems—is this: to be human is to be a consumer. That has come to apply to religion as well. It used to be that much of what religion meant had to do with being born, baptized into a family, a church that we grew up in. Living in a certain town, a neighborhood where our family had been for several generations, we breathed, we ate, and we slept certain values and judgments that were called Christian. Being religious was as natural as being a Smith, a Jones, a Hearst.

That's not true anymore. It used to be you could point to something like the Unification Church and call it a sect—something on the fringe, the margin. Now, *anything* called religion is on the margin. They're all sects, in a way. It means no more to be an Episcopalian than to be a Foursquare Gospeller, a Pentecostal Holiness member, a Seventh Day Adventist, a Jehovah's Witness—or, for that matter, a Hare Krishna or a Moonie. They're all the same. This is a pluralistic society and the public dimension of religion tends to be ignored. Religion becomes a private affair and the supermarket is the model. You walk down the aisles and you decide which one you'd like to try. Religion was never like that before. In this consumer world, the people will have a try at the Moonies even before they look to Anglicanism. It's all there on the shelves together, and the management isn't pushing any particular brand.

I realize this letter is getting a bit long, but I'm on a roll. Read it in shifts, if you must. Anyhow, I can't leave things in the lurch. I'm sure you're anxious to point out that so far I haven't really said much about the Moonies. I've talked around them. So let me see whether I can give you a bit of an insight into them. I've studied their literature and I've been to some of their conferences. If you promise not to tell anyone—I'll admit that I've served them as a consultant, delivered papers on subjects of interest to them. I've even written for some of their publications. For some strange reason, I have a difficult time remembering what I learn of their theory and practice. It doesn't stay with me very long. That's partly because much of the teaching awaits those who are prepared to come inside, to be disciples. I should say, I see nothing wrong with that. Would that it were more true of Catholic Christianity, especially of our own Anglicanism. Remembering their doctrine is also difficult because it's a new religion. It hasn't worked out the kinks yet. But it's been moving fast. It's way ahead of the Latter-Day Saints in working out its theology. The Saints have only started taking theology seriously in the last twenty years, and they've been around since 1830, or thereabouts.

Be all that as it may, explaining Unification doctrine isn't easy. First of all, the name—the official name is "Holy Spirit Association for the Unification of World Christianity." Like the Mormons, the Moonies see their movement as the restoration of a true Christianity, but unlike the Mormons, the Moonies see the Unification movement as fulfilling the purpose of all religions. It claims that all Christians must be united in a mood of expectancy, waiting for the restoration of God's original creative intention. Now, of course, according to Unificationism, traditional Christianity has misinterpreted much of God's intention—especially since the crucifixion of Jesus forced us to try to figure out what happened to the divine plan. You see, according to this point of view, the crucifixion represents—well, not exactly a failure, but the thwarting of God's purposes. For us, for the Catholic Christian tradition, the crucifixion and resurrection are central to God's revelation. In that double event we encounter a reality we would not otherwise know about. Not so for Unificationism.

Let me see whether I can reconstruct the Christian story according to the Unification understanding of it. Everything that exists has an internal character and a visible external form. The internal is Sung Sang; the external is Hyung Sang—both Korean terms. This is a kind of dualism—two-sidedness—that is true of God, too, as creator. Because of this two-sidedness, existence is a kind of give-and-take action, first giving, then receiving, which is meant to keep things in proper union, balance. Harmony exists when Sung Sang and Hyung Sang are in give-and-take balance. Humankind was created as a giving on the part of God, which humans must receive, then *give* in return. Each of us is capable of what Unificationism calls the First Blessing, the ability to live harmoniously with oneself and with God. If we accomplish this we are able to receive God's love, to become perfect individuals who, then, as husband and wife, can unite in give-and-take action that gives birth to sinless children. This is the Second Blessing. And it gives rise to the third—a world in which God and humanity, humanity and cosmos and nature, are in complete harmony.

Ah, but something happened to distort this scheme, says Unificationism. Christians call it the Fall, but Unificationists have a different interpretation from the orthodox view. You see, in the perfection of Paradise (Eden), Adam and Eve were supposed to achieve the first blessing (growing into perfection as individuals) as brother and sister. Then they would have moved to the Second Blessing and become the original True Parents, creating God's family of sinless humanity. But Eve gave in to intercourse with Satan, then seduced Adam into sexual union before—you see, this is what's important—*before* the First Blessing was accomplished. Therefore, the Third Blessing of a harmonious world became impossible. However, God is not to be thwarted. He will achieve his purposes. He has provided dispensation after dispensation, down through history, for the three blessings to be realized.

Jesus was the Messiah, the one who was to become the first True Parent since the Fall. He achieved the First Blessing and became the true Son, object of God's love. However, he was misunderstood; and there were those who were successful in preventing him from finding the other true parent with whom he could have united in divine marriage to create the sinless family of God.

We are now living in days which may well be the time of the Third Adam, the Lord of the Second Advent. Christ will come as a man in the flesh and will establish a family through marriage to his Bride, a woman in the flesh. If we obey the True Parents, our original sin will be eliminated and we will achieve the first blessing ourselves and begin true families. The day is now at hand, says Unification teaching.

While we await the coming of the Messiah, our true Parent, we have to meet certain conditions. We have to pay indemnity for what was lost when Adam fell. The Messiah cannot come until we prepare for him properly. The concept of indemnity is not at all clear in Unification thought. At one point it speaks of paying, indemnifying, in such a way that specific conditions must be met—almost like an eye for an eye, a tooth for a tooth. At other times, all that the concept seems to mean is that somehow we must pay for Adam's faithlessness by rallying around someone who demonstrates perfect faith and knows how to love others without jealousy.

This whole business is quite complex and still undeveloped at some stages of thinking. But, of course, if the day is "at hand" for the Lord of the Second Advent, it must mean that conditions are ready for his coming. And it won't be the theology, the doctrine, that's important, but the readiness of people to accept and obey the True Parents.

Unification doctrine is known as the *Divine Principle* and was revealed to Sun Myung Moon sometime before the end of World War II. Moon is a Korean, born in 1920, whose parents became Presbyterian converts in 1930. Now, Korea is one of the few places in Asia that has experienced widespread conversion to Christianity in modern times. The Koreans are an emotional and individualistic people. The country is alive religiously. It is primarily evangelical in its Christianity, but the Roman Catholic Church is also strong. And in the midst of it all are elements of folk religion and shamanism, Confucianism, Taoism, and Buddhism. After all, Korea is also the land from which Buddhism entered Japan in the sixth century. But the one big spiritual factor in the life of modern Korea is the great quasi-religion of Communism.

All this is background for understanding the experience of Sun Myung Moon. On Easter Sunday of 1936, when he was sixteen, Moon reported later, Jesus appeared to him and told him he was chosen to attempt the completion of Jesus' mission. Between that time and the beginning of his mission in 1946, he kept quiet about the revelation experience, discovered the Principle, and watched the rising tide of Communism. He spent two years in a gulag until his liberation by U.N. forces in 1950. The first missionary of the movement came to America in 1959; Moon himself arrived in Washington, D.C., in December of 1971.

My dear Lydia, I fear I have bored you with the recitation of Moonie doctrine and reference to the life of the Reverend Sun Myung Moon. Perhaps you aren't really interested in these details. Would you forgive me if I told you that I don't think you're not all that worried about your nephew and his espousal of the Moonies? Isn't it that—well, you know—his joining the Moonies seems like the end of the world? I mean, *your* world, *my* world—the comfortable world that was still with us when we were kids, but started disintegrating after the Second World War. The Moonies represent an unknown, an exotic departure from the mainstream. If your nephew had become a Methodist, you wouldn't worry...well, you might worry a little bit. But Randy took up with a religion which seems like a "cult"—it's different, it's strange, it's a bit bizarre to you. It's not in harmony with those "common essentials" that religion in America is supposed to share.

America had the same response to the Latter-Day Saints in the last century. The mainstream thought the Mormons would undermine the entire American culture. They were persecuted. What we didn't understand was that the Mormons were more American than America itself. But basically we distrusted them because they taught a strange brand of Christianity and had some curious marital practices. (Of course, so do the rest of us, but we don't know what to do about it.) So the emergence of Mormonism in the nineteenth century is the beginning of modernity in American religion. It spells the eventual collapse of the "common essentials" and the end of the Christian era.

The Moonies believe that marriage created on love and desire is based on the same illicit love that caused the fall of Adam and Eve. Remember, marriage is to create the true family of God and can only be entered into by those whose lives are centered on God. Only the True Parent can restore marriage to God's love by arranging those marriages himself.

I said, my dear Lydia, that you are worried about your own world being threatened. You see, when a person joins a movement like Unificationism, he gives us a signal. He tells us that we have no convictions that make a difference. He tells us that belonging to a meaningful community that has the courage to require something of its people—that's what's important. I've studied religion long enough to think that it's not the doctrine itself that is the first attraction to a religion. People will learn whatever doctrine they need to if they see a community that is vital, living, and supportive. Why? Because it's the community, the strength of it, that attracts. It's sort of like being drawn to a charismatic person. You say to yourself—Hey! that person must have something! I'll listen to whatever she says. I want to be like that! I like to be near her.

Dear Lydia, I think the members of St. Woebegone's may have to decide whether they have the courage to discover the revolution at the foundation of our own tradition. Isn't it time—especially in this age—for us to say to each other: this is what we believe, this is what we think, this is what we do. We know who we are! Everybody who belongs to this community must know what it means, must accept discipline, and be prepared to have it make a difference.

In one of Isaac Singer's short stories, Rabbi Gabriel Klintower has just finished the periods of mourning for his deceased wife, Menucha Alte. He has been wrestling with persistent and unbridled passions. After all, his wife had been a saint, yet she lived in torment. And he, Rabbi Gabriel, could think of nothing but naked women. Yet here he was, healthy and surviving. The righteousness of God made no sense. Actually, the Almighty had never answered Job's questions. All he had done was to boast about His wisdom and His might.

Rabbi Gabriel was demoralized. He couldn't keep on teaching. He stopped in the middle of his lectures and turned over the leadership of the Hasidim to his son. But his son was weak and the yeshiva went untended.

Then one night Rabbi Gabriel had a dream. He was a bridegroom being led to the wedding canopy with Menucha Alte. She was so beautiful he was overcome with astonishment. She was like an angel; even her veil and gown shone with a special radiance. The Hasidim were singing, yeshiva students were studying the Talmud, and the women were dancing. The world seemed in order, redemption drawn near.

When he awoke, Rabbi Gabriel washed his hands, dressed, and set out for the study house. "What else can I do?" he asked himself. "Everything is as it should be. Should I go to the tavern, to a house of ill repute? No." He had awakened with new vigor and a dedication to learning.

A cheder boy was walking toward him, carrying a Pentateuch and a paper bag of food. Rabbi Gabriel stopped him. "Do you want to earn two groschen?" he asked.

"Yes, Rabbi."

"What should a Jew do who has lost the world to come?"

The boy seemed to ponder. "Be a Jew."

"Even though he has lost the world to come?"

"Yes."

"And study Torah?"

"Yes."

"Since he is lost, why the Torah?"

"It's good."

"It's good, eh? As good as candy?"

The boy hesitated a moment. "Yes."

"Well, you just earned two groschen." He bent down, pinched the boy's cheek and kissed his forehead. "You are cleverer than all of them. Go and buy yourself some sweets." The boy grabbed the coin and ran. And Rabbi Gabriel went straight to the yeshiva. When the students saw the rabbi, they were very surprised to see him back. They stood up in awe. Rabbi Gabriel shouted, " The boy knows the truth!" And he began to lecture at the place he had left off weeks before.[†]

The truth is what it is! You must learn to abide in it even if you are living in a woebegone world that praises existence as one damned thing after another. You study, you pray, you chant the divine sounds of the universe, and you do what you have to do. You know the truth! The truth is, there is nothing honorable left to do! When your nephew joined the Moonies, he was looking for that honorable thing that we couldn't help him find because we didn't stand by what we know.

I think there's another reason for the success of the Moonies. Maybe your nephew caught the vision of the kingdom of God. The Unification movement believes that the kingdom must come on earth. They must build it even though it is God's kingdom. And it is urgent that they build it on earth, because if they don't, the Communists will succeed in building the kingdom of Satan, which will delay God's plan. The kingdom of God in heaven awaits the realization of the kingdom of God on earth. This means political, economic, and educational work. It explains why the Moonies are constantly involved in business ventures that the rest of us resent—of which we are suspicious. They are preparing the kingdom on earth

---

[†] Adapted from Isaac Bashevis Singer, *Old Love* (New York: Farrar Straus & Giroux, 1979), pp. 147-148.

for the Lord of the Second Advent. Hard work for the kingdom! Now, whether you like it or not, it's a vision that is missing from much of our society, held together by a corporate bureaucracy that feeds on the sanctification of self-gratification.

I'm sure I've raised more questions than I've answered. But that's okay. Let me just say two more things. Unificationism is a modern religious movement. It's a reaction against a world that sells its soul to the notions of a false rationality, a world that promises salvation through conformity and gadgetry. In such a world, I'm glad that some intelligent young people turn to the Moonies. Perhaps it'll make the rest of us sit up and take stock.

Having said that, I'll add a sobering thought. Strange as it may seem after all I've already said: I don't know that Unificationism will be around too long. It's too idealistic, in one sense; its followers are dreamy-eyed intellectuals. And it's too complicated and cerebral a system for most Americans. Perhaps it's not even a true religion, but more like a philosophy. Americans are not intellectuals, especially not when it comes to religion. Americans want quick answers, success, and comfort. And they never want to be accused of being fanatics, especially not the men, who leave the spiritual future of humanity to the dedication of women. Gosh, I hadn't thought of it: Maybe there lies our salvation. Have a go at it, Lydia.

There's a Hasidic story about how the world averted catastrophe, when it had already been decreed that patience had run out and the end was imminent.

"Why was disaster averted?" asked the Baal Shem Tov. "I'll tell you: it had nothing to do with our efforts—yours and mine. It wasn't the great sages or the great spiritual leaders. Our litanies, our fasting, were all in vain. We were saved by a woman.

" This is how it happened: she came to the synagogue, tears running down her face, and addressed the almighty: 'Master of the Universe, are you or are you not our Father? Why won't you listen to your children imploring you? You see, I'm a mother. Children I have plenty of: five. And every time they shed a tear, it breaks my heart. But you, Father, you have so many more. Every person is your child, and every one of them is weeping and weeping. Even if your heart is made of stone, how can You remain indifferent?' And God decided she was right."[†]

Yours in Christ

[†] Elie Wiesel, *Souls on Fire* (New York: Vintage Books, 1973), p. 44.

"When You're All Stressed Out"

Dear Nora,

So how are things at St. Woebegone's? Really, I mean. As you know, I haven't been around for awhile. Maybe it's just as well. Sometimes it's necessary to get away from all those things that bother people so much. I mean, why can't we just let St. Woebegone's be woebegone? Perhaps that sounds a bit callous. I don't know. Sometimes I get the idea that even Jesus was saying, "Hey! Just go and sin no more! Sin! Sin! Sin! I'm tired of hearing about it. Do something else!" Anyhow, I had to get away from focusing all my attention on "spiritual problems" and the concern for the trimming of fat that may be taking place in the church.

It seems a terrible thing to say, but there is this woman who corners me every so often. She always unloads her burdens. The other day it took two hours. I had to listen to all the mean things her relatives were saying about her. She finally got up to leave.

"Well, Father," she said, "when I came in here I had a terrible headache, like a migraine. But now, thanks to you, it's gone."

I wanted to say, "Mrs. Smith, your headache isn't gone at all. I have it now."

But maybe that's okay. Something had to happen to the headache.

I read your letter over several times. I guess it helped me to see that Mrs. Smith (I'll call her) has to do something with her headaches. So what can I say to her: "Keep them, I'm not interested"? Stress is the word we hear so much of these days. What do you do when you're all stressed out? That's *your* question, but it seems to be the question of a lot of folks at St. Woebegone's. I suppose that's why some of us agreed to call dear old St. Agnes' "St. Woebegone's." Everyone seems to be so despondent. And so many people say they aren't getting anything from the church to help their despair and their stress.

Well, of course, we ought to do a better job of leaving our headaches on the altar. That's trite, but true enough. But for some reason, we're not. And people—members of the church—are turning to all kinds of guide books and how-to books. They're going to "stress-management" seminars and they're taking vitamins that are fortified against "stress." Churches like the Crystal Cathe-

dral in Garden Grove, California, are built on spiritual stress-management formulas. Robert
Schuller has become an international celebrity, a
best-selling author—probably a millionaire—with
a ministry based upon the nurture of "self-
esteem." A recent Gallup poll discovered that
three in ten Americans have a low sense of self-
worth. Sometimes it doesn't make sense to me.
How can a society that sanctifies greed be lacking
in self-esteem? A consumerist society such as
ours promotes the satisfaction and pleasure of
the private self at the expense of everything else.
Now, I realize that stress and low self-esteem are
not the same thing. But they're related.

There is no doubt in my mind that stress is
spiritual, a religious matter. It's more than being
faced with a job that's too demanding. Stress is
finding yourself living in a world that expects you
and me to do its bidding. Stress occurs when "the
world" sends a message that says, "You, my
daughter, are income tax and mortgages. You are
a real estate broker. That is who you are. Your
worth is measured by how much work you can
put out and how much money you can earn, and
how many things you can buy." "The world"
sends that message.

But something else whispers, "There's no way
you can measure up. You can't make it. There
isn't enough time. And I'm not so sure you have
what it takes."

And into that conversation there comes
another word: It is a weeping word, a compassionate word. It cries: "Is that *all* you are? Is
that what life is all about? I can see why you live
in stress, if that's all you think you are. Because I
understand, I understand that you constantly

have to meet the expectations you have for your-self—that the world holds out for you. You have to meet those expectations because that's all there is. If that's all there is, then you just have to accept the stress and its consequences!"

Now, of course, I realize that a lot of the stress in this world is not that kind of stress. It's the frustration of driving a car in feverish traffic, of trying to find a parking place. Stress is trying to make ends meet, trying to live with a teenager, or with a husband who's never home when you need him. But are those issues really so different from the stress of "measuring up" in a world that tries to capitalize on your self-esteem even as it main-tains a very low opinion of what it means to be human? Aren't all these stressful circumstances the result of living in a world that bluffs you into believing you can and should somehow control life, you can handle it, manage it—by yourself—when your experience is just the opposite?

The messages of our consumerist society are filled with the illusions and fantasies of life as manageable, controllable, when in fact it isn't. The most popular courses and workshops are "management" courses. Life is fundamentally *un*-manageable! That's the glory of it. Life is the play-ful celebration of freedom. The playfulness of life can be ordered, but it can't be managed. The more it becomes an affair of management, the less human it becomes. The less human it be-comes, the more we succumb to the illusion that life is manageable. And so life is a rolling hoop made by the dragon eating his tail.

Order is different from management. An ordered life is lived by the person who knows he is part of a meaningful story that doesn't depend upon his ambitions or his successful management of things. All the story needs is telling. The order is part of the story. The story provides the order. Let me tell you something, Nora (a good spiritual director would never say this, but I'm not a good one, so I'll say it): you and your friends at St. Woebegone's want less stress in your lives? Be storytellers. Learn to tell stories. I mean it. Learn to tell the story of your life as part of a bigger story—a story with a mystery ending. I'm serious. I will guarantee what no spiritual director should say: Your life will get rid of its stress to the extent that you become a storyteller who tells stories as part of the mystery story of human existence.

A story, a long story: Saint Peter loved Jesus, said the Basque country people. Loved him but he couldn't figure him out. One time they were traveling together in Spain. They walked up and down the roads, feeling the soft dust between their toes every time they picked up their sandals. They named towns, founded churches, baptized babies, and did a lot of good.

Early one morning, they came across this farmer on the road. His wagon had hit a rock, tipped over on its side. His vegetables, wheat, his wine kegs, cheese gourds, everything, just lay spilled all over the road and in the ditch.

What a mess! But the farmer, he seemed calm about it all. He was a big, fat fellow. He was down on his knees, hands clasped together. Eyes closed. He was praying. "Lord Jesus," he was saying, not very loud. Strange he was praying that way. He had no idea that Jesus and St. Peter were coming up right behind him. "This is just what I deserve," he prayed. "I am a careless, miserable sinner. I could have seen that big rock in the middle of the road, but I wasn't watching. But I don't want to complain about it. I'm going to be grateful for all the good things that have happened to me. Praise God."

Well, Saint Peter was impressed. "Remarkable!" he said to the Lord Jesus. "What a healthy, humble fellow. Let's give him a hand, get all his goods back in his wagon."

Jesus looked straight ahead. "Keep walking," he said.

"But Lord," said St. Peter.

"Hush," said Jesus, "keep walking." Well, they went right by this unfortunate man, right on down the road. St. Peter, he kept stumbling along, kept looking back until Jesus told him to stop it.

They hadn't gone but a short distance until they came upon the same sight all over again. Another wagon was in a ditch. This time a whole side of the wagon was smashed in. A big load of wood and hay, thrown every which way. This farmer was on his knees, too, but he wasn't praying. He was swearing a blue streak. He had one bony shoulder jammed under one side of the wagon-bed, trying to rock the wagon up out of the ditch. He was sweating and straining and swearing. Nothing was happening.

This fellow was a kind of lean, mean sort. Tough. Scars on his face and hands. Long, crooked nose, all squashed and twisted. And that swearing. Something else. Saint Peter was bewildered. This man was sending one miserable curse after another out upon the innocent world. They didn't even make sense, thought St. Peter, being all about highways that ate manure and haywagons that slept with their mothers. St. Peter, he was really put off by it all.

"Don't stop," he whispered to Jesus. Jesus stopped.

"Lord, we better leave this man alone." Jesus stood right by him, looking down. "What are you doing?" asked Jesus. Not a very smart thing to ask.

Well, the farmer looked up, wiped the sweat out of his eyes. "The hell you mean, what am I doing? What's it look like?"

"In trouble, eh?"

The farmer got up slowly. Lean and stringy, big and mean. "If I am, I don't need you to tell me, now do I? So get moving!" And he cursed Jesus roundly. St. Peter couldn't believe his eyes. Then Jesus hauled off and socked that farmer. Really belted him one. Knocked him flat. The Lord Jesus Christ did that.

Well, St. Peter just knew this couldn't be happening. I mean, if Jesus said it once, he said it a thousand times: *Don't hit other people!* Just don't. And here he himself laid this farmer out cold. St. Peter put a hand over his face, and shook his head. When he looked again, he saw Jesus down on one knee. He was poking one end of his walking stick under the wagon bed. Jesus glanced at the farmer lying there, out cold, and he chuckled. He stood up, pushing on the little stick. And the wagon rocked right out of the ditch, rolled onto the road and stopped. It stood right side up, axles straight. There wasn't a mark on the side that was smashed. All the wood and hay was back where it had been. "There!" said Jesus and started walking down the road. St. Peter stared at the wagon and the unconscious farmer. He rubbed his head and ran after Jesus, who didn't want to talk about it.

Now St. Peter was a good man, you know, for the most part. But he had to be certain about every little thing in his mind, or he worried. He was brave as a lion when he knew what the trouble was. But when he wasn't sure, he was under a lot of stress. I mean, if someone near him acted cold, he worried. If someone seemed disappointed, he worried. And if he saw somebody laughing, and couldn't figure out why, he thought he was the one being laughed at, and the more such things happened, the more stressful he became, and he fidgeted about making all kinds of excuses. That's what Jesus enjoyed about St. Peter. He liked kidding him about his worrying, never got tired of it.

Take the first time St. Peter took Jesus fishing. I mean, St. Peter was a fisherman. He knew all about such things and he knew where the big schools of fish would run in the Sea of Galilee that day. He had Jesus up and into his boat before dawn. They were the first ones out of the harbor. St. Peter, he stood up in his boat and called to the other fishermen, "Follow me!" I mean, he was out to show Jesus how the professionals did it.

So out they went, the other boats following. Right out into the middle of the Sea of Galilee. Nothing but water all around. St. Peter slacked his sail, stood up, sniffed the air, slid one hand quietly over the water, tasted a finger. The other boats glided silently around him. St. Peter pointed to a spot about a hundred feet to the left. "There!" he said quietly. The nets went out, easily. They weren't thrown. Jesus watched with interest.

"Why don't we throw the nets?" whispered Jesus.

"Because there are so many fish down there, we don't want to scare them." It was true. There were.

"Oh," said Jesus. He looked down into the water, tapped the edge of the boat with his walking stick, softly. No one saw. More fish than anyone could count dived straight to the bottom of the Sea of Galilee. The nets were pulled through the water, over and over, up and down. They came up empty. Not one fish.

Well, St. Peter, he started rubbing his head. He was getting nervous. His boat was soon surrounded by other boats, full of angry professional fishermen. They called St. Peter, in no uncertain terms, a damned blockhead. They mumbled and swore about half a day wasted and sailed off. St. Peter went over his calculations. He'd never been *that* wrong before. He inspected the nets. Not a hole anywhere. He couldn't figure out what happened.

Jesus, he said fishing was sure an interesting profession. That made St. Peter feel very strange—all stressed out.

Which is exactly the way he felt now, running after Jesus down the road, just after Jesus had knocked out that mean farmer, and then fixed the wagon for him. "Lord, wait a minute!" he shouted.

So Jesus turned around and came back to him. "Well?"

St. Peter counted it off on his fingers. "One farmer in a ditch prays to you. You pass him by. Another farmer in a ditch swears at you. You do to him what you plainly tell every Christian *never* to do to anybody, and *then* you save the fellow's neck by pulling his wagon out of the ditch."

"Well?"

"I don't understand. What was so *bad* about the first farmer? What was so *good* about the second farmer? If something was so *good* about the second farmer, and not about the first farmer, why hit the second farmer before helping him? It makes no sense to me."

"So *try*," said Jesus. It was getting close to noon, and hot. Jesus saw a shade tree a few yards off. He laid down beneath its branches, ate a pear from his sack, and took a nap. While St. Peter *tried*. He rubbed his head. He paced around in circles, figured things this way and that, drew them up in different ways, knocked his fist against his palm. I mean, he thought about it every which way, and he was all stirred up.

When Jesus got awake, St. Peter was ready for him. "Lord, I understand."

"Good," said Jesus. He yawned.

"A decent man's curse is better than a shifty man's prayer."

It sounded good. Jesus seemed impressed.

"That's it. Isn't it?"

Jesus complimented St. Peter on his powers of deduction. St. Peter blushed with pride and pleasure. Jesus yawned again. And St. Peter felt a spasm of doubt come over him.

"Wait!" he said. "If that second farmer was so decent, and the first farmer wasn't, then why hit the second farmer and not the first one?"

Jesus stretched and shook himself awake.

St. Peter went on: "Because if the second farmer was too proud to be helped, which is possible, and had to be put to sleep so you could help him, which is reasonable, then why was he worth helping in the first place, him being proud? And if the first farmer..."

But Jesus was already off down the road again. His step was light and bouncy. He was feeling good about the pleasant afternoon, and wasn't going to say any more about it.

St. Peter felt very strange again. He ran down the road after Jesus, thinking as he ran. He rubbed his head, and scratched his head, and rubbed his head, and scratched it.

That is how St. Peter got so bald so young.[†]

Now Nora, I know I should just leave you with that story. It's bad policy to interpret a good story like that. You risk getting too preachy. But I can't resist the temptation. We could say a lot of things about the story itself. We could draw a moral that says, "Look at St. Peter. He was a worry wart. Lost his hair trying to figure everything out. He was a person who just couldn't let loose ends lie. He was a control person. And it was mighty stressful. Jesus, on the other hand, he just did what he had to do, didn't think much about it afterward. He took a nap and he bounced on down the road in the afternoon sun."

The only problem with that is the same problem I have with most stories that have a moral—I want to ask, "So what?" I mean, so St. Peter was a stressful guy and Jesus wasn't. Do you think St. Peter can change just because we tell him he'd

---

[†] Adapted from Romulus Linney, *Jesus Tales* (Berkeley, CA: North Point Press, 1987), pp. 3-9.

better change, or he'll lose all his hair? Well, I don't think so. That's why I can't understand how some people can sit and listen to some sermons. A lot of sermons end up saying, "Don't be like St. Peter. Be more like Jesus." And the people leave the church, pleased that someone told them something like that. The preacher shared a moral lesson. Big deal! What we need to hear about is how a fidgety person like St. Peter can learn to live with the fidgets. Once he learns to live with the fidgets, he's cured. But you tell him he's got to stop being so fidgety and he's going to get mighty fidgety.

What I have been trying to say is that telling stories is the way to learn how to avoid stress. The story of St. Peter and Jesus does not tell us that we *must* avoid stress. It doesn't give us any steps to follow. But I'll wager if you heard that story you would be smiling; and if you told it, you would find yourself ready to bounce down the road with Jesus. Why? Why is that so? Because the story is not a prescription, not a recipe, not a court summons. It's just something to be part of. A story like that is lifting you out of ordinary existence. Ordinary existence expects things of you. You expect things of yourself. It expects you to prove something. But a story says, hey! It's all bigger than anything you can prove. You don't need to prove anything. Just be yourself.

Have you ever thought why it is that born-again evangelicals often seem so happy? Well, partly it's because they can tell you a story about who they were, and what they were like, until they met Jesus, and who they are now. Telling the story is basic to their lives. A story always talks about meetings—meetings with people, meetings with God, with Buddha. A story is not a set of propositions or rules for improved behavior. It's always about people meeting. Life *is* a story. It's not propositions, rules, or information. It's a story, and the sooner you learn to tell the story, the better off you'll be.

Jesus was a storyteller. A person comes up to him, all stressed out. "What do I have to do?" he asks. "How can I find peace, eternity?" "Well, you have the law? What does it say?" The man recites the first and second commandments. "Right!" says Jesus, "That's it! There's your answer!" The man gets a bit nervous. "But tell me," he asks, "How do I do that?" Notice, Jesus doesn't answer, "Well, first you do this, then you do that." That would've made the man more fidgety. Jesus said, "Once upon a time a man was travelling from Jerusalem to Jericho..." Jesus told a story—that oft-told story of the Good Samaritan. And a story either grabs you or it doesn't. If it grabs you, you're lifted up, out of your feverish expectations. In that familiar story Jesus is really saying, "Hey! *Neighbors happen*! Be ready!"

What's the secret there? No prescription, no stress. No attachment to the need to be a good neighbor—something you already know. A man was mugged on the way to Jericho. A priest comes along, mumbling the words of the commandments: "I must set an example, set an example, set an example. I must be a good person, be a good person, be a good person. I must show the people, show the people, show the people. I hope they like me when I offer the sacrifices, offer the sacrifices, offer the sacrifices. Say! What's that fellow doing lying there in the gutter? Gosh! You see a little bit of everything these days. Probably dead from too much wine. Not much anybody can do!" On he goes.

Not far behind is his curate, on his way to a pro-choice rally. "Old Fr. Saltzman, he's just not with it," mumbles the curate. "He doesn't see God announcing his liberation of all people. All he cares about is budgets and morality. He never understands that God cares more about the homeless and the needy than he cares about whether someone plays hanky-panky with another woman's husband. Saltzman's a real bastard to work for! Wonder who that is lying in the ditch? I've got to get the committee on the homeless to work on these things. That's what the Gospel is all about!" On he goes.

Along comes this strange fellow, humming through his nose like Willie Nelson, "On the Road Again!" The man's a foreigner. Just bouncing along, singing. "Hey! What's this? I better give this poor son of a gun a hand. Looks as though he needs it. Hey you! Give me a hand with this fellow. Help me get him up on my mule!"

Now, Jesus has no problem with priests and Levites, or with commandments. But a priest who is too attached to his job is not a good priest. And if he's too attached to the commandments, he'll be uptight, tense—more interested in commandments than people. So Jesus avoids a stressful answer to the question of how to be a neighbor by telling a story instead of prescribing steps for being neighborly. And his story itself suggests that the person who doesn't try to be a Savior, who just lives out the story—will be the one who's ready to be a neighbor when necessary. He's not trying to prove anything, not even trying to be a good guy.

Of course, the only story that will really re-
move the stress from your life is one that's big
enough. There has to be a story that's more than
your private story. It has to be a story in which
you belong, big enough for you to work out your
own private story as an episode. It has to be
God's story. If it isn't, then you are responsible
for the whole story and that's mighty stressful.

You know, Nora, I think we need to get together just to tell stories to each other. We can
tell stories we've read or heard. We can tell about
things that've happened to us, things that we've
thought about. And we can learn again to tell the
" old, old story"—just to see where our own stories fit. I guarantee you, if we did that, there'd be
no stress in our lives.

Eric Hoffer was America's type of philosopher,
a migrant worker and longshoreman who read
everything he could get his hands on. And he
thought. He reflected. And he imagined. A special
sort of person. In his autobiographical memories
he talks about his discovery of the Old Testament
as a young man, while he was wandering from job
to job in the fields, placer mines, and restaurants
of California. He found the Old Testament. He
said that he had always figured it was a religious
book and since he wasn't particularly religious,
he'd never come across it or seen any reason to
pick it up.

Finally, curiosity got the better of him. He
read. And do you know what he said? " Life throbs
in every line of the book. The eager creativeness
of the imagination of the unequaled storytellers
is a goad to their powers of observation. Nothing
is too slight for their attention: motives, acts,
speech, dress, manners, and innumerable particu-

lars are rendered with great vividness. There is everywhere evident a love of everyday reality. The good is taken with the bad. There is no touching-up to lend a false appearance of perfect. The great men have faults, and these are recorded with as much vividness and detail as accomplishments and virtues. The imagined truth of these storytellers is more alive, more true, than truth."[†]

The Jews have been a people who accept life in its entirety, because it is God's world. You can argue with God if you are in his world, his story, but you don't get ulcers.

Nora, I must be tiring you out with all this chatter about story. But I wanted so desperately to avoid another "how-to" response to your concerns. You can write one of those "how-to" books yourself, even under stress. They will tell you that first you must figure out what kinds of situations are stressful to you. Then you must ask: Now, is any of this stress necessary? Is any of it acceptable? Can you do anything about the stress that is unacceptable to you? And I suppose all that makes sense. I recommend it. But isn't it a little bit like telling an amnesiac that she should familiarize herself with her hometown? You see, I don't believe that a person who takes the church seriously will have much of a problem with stress. Because I know that the secret to handling it is bound up with the story, the tradition, of our Catholic faith. A person who isn't getting any help from the church isn't looking for it. She isn't

[†] Eric Hoffer, *Truth Imagined* (New York: Harper & Row, 1983), p. 16.

going to someone and asking, "What must I do? What is there that the saints are getting and I'm not?"

After all, what is stress? It is the narrowing of personality, to the point where we are transformed into the image of our own demands and desires. When this happens, there is no way out. Stress is the only result because human beings are more than their own desires. The mind of Christ lurks beneath the lowered horizon of life.

Stress is a failure to recognize that the gap between expectation and fulfillment can never be bridged, but only accepted. The plot of all stories deals with that fact. And the story of stories is the key to acceptance. When you let God tell the story, the world lightens up.

Eric Hoffer tells the story of Johnny the bum. Johnny was always able to bamboozle people into feeding him without doing a lick of work. One day, as he was riding on top of a freight train, he suddenly got very hungry. When that sort of thing happened, he usually just got off the train and walked to the nearest farm. But in this part of northern California, the only farm in sight was that of the widow Jones. She had the reputation of being tough, never feeding a tramp unless he worked. But Johnny had no choice. He could hear the animals laughing as he came into the widow's farmyard. "Hey! Look who's coming!" The dog was jumping at the prospect of watching what would happen.

The widow answered Johnny's knock. She stood there with her ax in hand, pointed to a clump of trees, and said, "Here's the ax. Cut down those trees into firewood and I'll feed you." As Johnny started walking over to the trees, ax in hand, the dog jumping for joy, he heard the trees laughing. Saying: "Hey! Look at Johnny with the ax. Isn't that sidesplitting!" Johnny paused, the word "sidesplitting" in his ears. He knew God was with him. What he'd do was to tell the trees a funny story so they'd split their sides and all he'd have to do is pick up the pieces.

So he sat down under a tree, started telling a story about an immigrant who lived in California during the gold-rush days. Some of these people weren't allowed to mine gold-rich dirt but had to get what they could by washing tailings—that's mining jargon for leftover silt that may have some gold bits. When they ran out of tailings, this one fellow decided to be a woodcutter. He got himself an ax, knocked on a door. A woman opened the door, said, "Yes?"

"Me cut wood," replied the man. The woman answered, "How much?" He said, "Cut, chop, stack—three dollars a cord." "Oh," said the woman, "that's very nice. How much cut, chop, no stack?" The fellow counted on his fingers, "Two dollars, seventy cents." The woman smiled, "How much cut, no chop, no stack?" The poor fellow counted on his fingers again, "Two dollars a cord." "Wonderful," said the woman. "How much no cut, no chop, no stack?"

The immigrant started counting on his fingers and became very confused. So he started again, finally burst out, "You plenty strange woman!"

Well, the trees laughed so hard they shook, split their sides, so Johnny started gathering the pieces and headed back to the farmhouse. Then he noticed one tree left standing. So he asked the dog, "What's the matter with that tree?" "Oh," said the dog, "that's an *English* walnut tree."

Johnny shook his head and started to walk away. About a hundred yards on he heard a big noise behind him. He turned to look: the English walnut tree was splitting its side.[†]

No stress in Johnny's world, Nora. Life is a story. Live it and laugh, splitting your sides.

Yours in Christ

[†] Adapted from *Truth Imagined*, pp. 57-58.

"When Your Business Has No Time For Ethics"

Dear Anthony,

Your letter reached me some time ago. I hesitated to answer. The issue you raise is one of the most complex of problems we face today. Ethics! The ethics of a techno-corporate world. I really don't know exactly how to deal with it. I know that this world has no time for ethics. We only have time for business! Now, that sounds very cynical, even pessimistic, I suppose. And recently I've been accused of being a pessimist by some first-rate optimists. But I'm not really a pessimist. Nor am I an optimist, for that matter. The pessimist and the optimist suffer from the same Western malaise. They both live in the same perception of the world. They believe that the future *depends upon the possibility* of manipulating the world to a state of perfection. The pessimist believes it is impossible; the optimist believes it's inevitable.

I personally don't live in that kind of world. I live in a world in which human beings do what they have to do. I am not surprised by evil, because it resides in me, and I am not dependent upon success or utopia. Like C. S. Lewis, I am visited by "joy" in the most ordinary of circumstances. When T. S. Eliot spoke to the boys at Milton Academy in 1933, he told them they should not admire or hope for success, because it would feel just the same as failure. Instead, they should discover the right thing to do and then do it.

The thought is similar to what I read in a novel entitled *The Three-Cornered World* by the Japanese writer, Natsume Soseki. "Approach everything rationally," he wrote, "and you become harsh. Pole along in the stream of emotions, and you will be swept away by the current. Give free rein to your desires, and you become uncomfortably confined. It is not a very agreeable place to live, this world of ours. When the unpleasantness increases, you want to draw yourself up to some place where life is easier. It is just at the point when you first realize that life will be no more agreeable no matter what heights you may attain, that a poem may be given birth, or a picture created."

I happen to agree with Soseki's aesthetic. It is the business of the artist to create a beautiful picture just to be enjoyed. We need to be able to see something beautiful in the midst of rather dour circumstances.

"After thirty years in this world of ours," says one of Soseki's characters, "I have had more than enough of the suffering, anger, belligerence and sadness which are ever present; and I find it very trying to be subjected to repeated doses of stimulants designed to evoke these emotions when I go to the theatre, or read a novel."

Help me to live, says Soseki! Help me to live in this world. But don't *drag me through it.*

"The poet and the artist...come to know absolute purity by concerning themselves only with those things which constitute the innermost essence of this world of relativity. They dine on the summer haze, and drink the evening dew."[†]

Soseki reminds us of a very important theological principle—that we must acquire the proper perception to see the world as it really is. We must be given eyes to see and ears to hear. We have to be in but not of the world. The good artist performs this task because he is concerned with the world, but not attached to its ordinary ways of perceiving. He creates perception. He makes a kind of beauty; and that is art.

The Christian story is a beautiful work of art. The artist is God himself, who says, "And then they took the man and dragged him up the hill. Get the picture. But he saw only the sunrise through the shuddering darkness. And after all

---

[†] Natsume Soseki, *The Three-Cornered World* (New York: G. P. Putnam's Sons, 1982), pp. 12, 19, 86-87.

the bloody ugliness of it all, there was honey-suckle on the morning breeze and the suffering was not the final word. Let me show you a beautiful picture of life that is stronger than death! Let me show what is on my heart."

You see, Anthony, I think the person who loves that picture, that story, knows how to walk in beauty in a world that is otherwise very disagreeable. Of course, there are those who tell us that one person's beauty is another person's horror. I'm sorry, I can't live with that! Some things are beautiful, other things aren't. And if you want to talk about beauty or walk in it, you've got to *contemplate* it, *learn* to see it.

There are people in this world who will steal a beautiful work of art in order to *sell* it, others who tack up laser landscapes and gaudy pink flamingoes. And so it is with religion. It is all one and the same, say those who have no standards; and they flutter piously about in this world making laser-landscape and pink-flamingo religion while the venerable beauty of the Catholic Church goes unseen.

Even those of us who have been raised in the Christian story as it is told in that liturgy and tradition may lose the perception it offers; nevertheless, it is like Soseki's work of art. It is a way of walking in beauty—as the Navajo says. It provides the possibility of living in the feverish world of business without being reduced to its silly attachments. And that's an important starting point as you begin to think about ethics. But now, on to something else.

No time for ethics, you say. Not only is there no *time* for it, but business operates with a set of rather ruthless assumptions that may be quite unethical. After all, business is in and of the world. I wouldn't ordinarily expect anything more of it. But before you get angry with me for saying that, let's unpack this matter of ethics. Ethics has to do with ethos—that which distinguishes the life of a particular group, a people. So ethics are the standards of conduct and responsible behavior characteristic of a people. If there were only one person in this world, there would be no ethics. Ethics are necessary because no person is an island. There must be standards of behavior to regulate, to keep our life together peaceful and just. And, of course, if we were residents of the Garden of Eden, there would also be no need for ethics. Once we have lost our innocence, and all of us have, then we live in a world where we are plagued by the knowledge of good and evil, right from wrong, foes from friends. And we worry about why the rain falls on the just. So, we have to establish two points: 1) ethics are necessary because life together must have standards; and 2) ethics are necessary because we do not live a life of innocence.

I once heard a student ask Jerry Falwell why he wanted to force his ethics upon others; why couldn't each person form her own code of ethics? Well, I was sympathetic to the student because she was challenging Falwell, but I have to admit that Falwell makes more sense than she did. The idea of ethics and the notion of "each person her own code" are mutually exclusive concepts. Each person her own code is anarchy and chaos. It isn't ethics because, you remember, ethics is the ordering of life together. Ethics is by nature a community venture, an inter-personal enterprise.

So now, if we have some conception of what we mean when we talk about ethics, let's go back to your original concern, friend Anthony. You said: "I work in a rough and tumble world. I spend a hectic week at it, week after week. And my business leaves no time for ethics. I have to sell what I have to sell, to whomever I can and using whatever means are necessary. I come to church on Sundays. I hear the priest talk about a kind of make-believe world, sort of like seeing a pretty picture, or reading a poem. But I know I won't have time for all that come Monday. The best I can do is feel better for a few minutes on Sunday. There have been many times when I've wanted to leave, to forget the church entirely. Maybe it's for people who have nothing better to do, for dreamers. Maybe it's all a scheme to get money out of people so that a few people can dream. It doesn't have a whole lot to do with my life. I'm a business person."

Your letter came about the time I was reading a volume of Isaac Singer's short stories. I know I've said it before, but I think Singer is a master magician, a master storyteller. If ever a person knew that life is a story, it's Isaac Singer. You're probably thinking: Who has time for stories? But hear me out. In one of the stories, called "The Secret," an elderly woman is talking about how a young man who was an apprentice in her husband's tailor shop became her lover. "One summer," she said, "on a Sabbath. It could never have happened in the middle of the week, since my husband worked at home. But on Sabbath afternoons he used to go with the tailors' group to study the *Pirke Aboth*, the *Ethics of the Fathers*.... By the time he came home, it was already late in the evening. I used to read in bed after the Sabbath meal. That day I had fallen into a deep sleep. I opened my eyes and Motke was lying beside me in bed. I wanted to scream in alarm, but he closed my mouth with his hand like an experienced rascal. This was a devil, not an apprentice."[†]

At first I thought about this business man who goes with his tailors' group on a Sabbath afternoon to study the *Pirke Aboth*. He's studying the system, the cases, the principles that help a Jew be an ethical tailor. And I asked, what's the difference? How come the tailor had time to study ethics? Well, it's because he wasn't permitted to *work* on the Sabbath. And he wasn't even allowed to watch television or play golf. So obviously his business knew there will be no ethics *unless* there is time for it. That's why we have the Sabbath in the first place. It is the ancient wisdom of the Jews—there will be no ethics unless there is time for it. The Sabbath is the time for it!

Think seriously about that creation story in the first chapter of Genesis. It's a story to penetrate. You have to say to yourself, I'm going to wiggle my way inside of this, see what's going on. God is very busy. He's making himself useful, doing this, doing that. Everything he does has function, a utility to it. It's business, doing what needs doing. Six days. On the sixth day he gave creation the eyes to see itself, the ears to hear,

---

[†] Isaac Bashevis Singer, *The Image and Other Stories* (New York: Farrar Straus & Giroux, 1985), p. 167.

the mind to conceive of itself—he created humankind!

Everything leading up to the creation of humankind is utilitarian, functional—business is business. But with the creation of male and female, he created more than business as usual. He made something in but not of this world—like himself. And so he rested. He did a very non-functional thing. He rested and he contemplated what he had done; and the human being that he created shared in that useless, non-business moment.

Now, what about the poor tailor who shared the contemplation of creation with God on the Sabbath? His apprentice seduced his wife while he made time for ethics. So should he have stayed at home? Well, I don't know. What do you think? Only you can decide whether his Sabbath-keeping was worth it. Do you want time for ethics, or don't you? Do you want to be reduced to business attachments, or would you like to know that you are more than all that?

In that same collection of stories is one called "A Nest Egg for Paradise." A wife often complained to her husband that if he hadn't spent so much time studying Hasidic lore and practice he could have found more prosperous sons-in-law for their daughters. But Reb Mendel would answer, "When a man reaches the world to come and is required to render accounts, the angel does not ask him how rich or how poor his sons-in-law are. He asks instead, 'Did you study Torah? Was your business honorable?'"[†]

Reb Mendel obviously believes that if a person really studies Torah, his business will be honorable. Torah, you see, is God sharing his contemplation of creation with us. That kind of study and contemplation are what make us human, give us honor, show we may be in but not of the business world. A business that has no time for ethics has no time for humanity. The less time we have for ethics, the less human will existence be. Because human existence is characterized by *choices*. Choices are made by free human beings who have studied and prayed about the ways of responsible choosing. If your business has no time for ethics, you had better begin some espionage, some sabotage of that business on behalf of human freedom, of human dignity and honor.

The fact that you tell me your business needs no time for ethics suggests that you may already know that your humanity requires more of you than your business demands. The first thing we must recognize and accept, of course, is the point I made earlier on: business is often an unethical enterprise that is symptomatic of the world in which we live. What we must continue to do is to accept that fact, find a way of living with it and subverting it.

Subversion begins with the Sabbath. It begins with that moment of satisfaction that contem-

[†] Singer, *The Image*, p. 177.

plates what has been done, places it in a much broader perspective than the number of sales made and the commissions reported. Sharing the mind of God in the Sabbath means that your Sabbath cannot be merely a time of golf or an afternoon on the lake. Such exercises in "recreation" are okay, but they are really part of the "business" of life. Observe, if you will, how much time, effort, and money are spent on radio, television, and newspaper commercials designed to attract you into places and kinds of "rest" and "recreation." Rest and recreation are part of the business—they are considered "functional." That is, they are *use*ful. Ethics needs a Sabbath. A Sabbath is a useless, nonfunctional day. It is like no other day. It's a day to move out of the world of business and function, a day to contemplate a commandment, to figure it out, to follow it into the world.

Alisha ben Abuyah used to go around visiting the study houses where the students pored over the Torah. "Out with you, you lazy people, stop idling away your days," he used to say. "Begin a practical work: *you* become a carpenter, and *you* a mason, *you* a tailor, and *you* a fisherman."[†] But to take a Sabbath is to find time for silence, for solitude, for useless study of the ways of the saints. It is a day like a work of art. It beautifies life, helps to see it with different eyes. A Sabbath is a time for prayer, meditation—perfectly useless ex-

[†] Abraham Joshua Heschel, *The Sabbath* (New York: Farrar Straus & Giroux, 1951), pp. 45-46.

penditures of time that will have a great deal to do with being a good carpenter, a mason, a tailor, a fisherman. That's what a human being is; like God, we must get outside our business. I know, some people say that prayer is very useful, that it can bring you success, peace of mind. Pay no attention to the promises. Just pray, study the saints, the great Christian classics, the Holy Scriptures. Just *do* it. I think Christians should start to go to Hebrew school. Study the Talmud, study the cases of the rabbis. There you can encounter interesting examples of what goes into ethical thinking. "You shall be holy because I am holy," say the Scriptures. Then it spells matters out in terms of everyday life.

For example, agriculture: "God made the world, He made things in a certain way, with a certain sense of order. Things should be whole, complete, fit naturally together." And so there are "laws" about the offerings to the priest, keeping seeds separate, a share of crops for the poor, and so on.

The Sabbath is for study and prayer. Very simple. Very useless. And I know of no other way to help us restore the dignity, the honor, restraint, and integrity that are the measure of a more human existence.

Why is the Sabbath important? Because it provides resources that you can't really do without and remain human. Ethics has to do with responsible interpersonal relations, remember? It has to do with actions and behavior. Your actions and behavior must be responsible to a God who expects you to be ready to be a neighbor. Well, now, there are so many actions that are done without decision, without reflection. It's impossible to weigh the circumstances of every action you take. Impossible! Often you don't really make a decision. You just act. Yet your actions are supposed to be responsible. Many decisions are "unconscious decisions." That means there must be resources at work in your life that affect your actions for the good, the responsible, the noble. They must be able to affect your unconscious decision-making. Those ethical resources are nurtured by a life that takes seriously the Sabbath—its attention to the useless activities of prayer and study. Without that attention, there are no resources and your life becomes less and less concerned with the ethical, your actions less responsible, and your life without dignity.

Now, let's move a few steps away. Let's recognize that many actions are the result of *conscious* decision. That's where certain questions must be raised and you have to be able to draw upon experience in working out responsible decisions. In these circumstances you must first be reminded of the purpose of life. To the Christian, life is an affair of recognizing the mind of Christ at work among us. Put another way, life is to be lived in such a way that the common good is served and that the common good is deified, that it should grow more Christlike and be raised above ordinary desire. We don't reduce life to the lowest common denominator, but raise it to its highest order. Before you go through any conscious decision-making, you have to ask yourself what life's purpose is and how the decisions you make will effect that purpose.

Another thing to remember is this: some of the most innocent decisions you make may be evil or have evil results. You have to realize that, and be able to recognize it. That's why the liturgy of the church has a prayer of confession that helps us to say: "We have left undone those things which we ought to have done [and there are ever so many of these]; and we have done those things which we ought not to have done." You see, Anthony, that's the *condition* of our existence, not just the happenstance of a bad week.

If you want a realistic understanding of life, you must accept the fact of existence as a condition of sinfulness. That will give your ethics a sense of preparedness. You won't expect too much of yourself or of others. No matter how serious you are in your ethics, you are not going to build the Kingdom of God. Often you will find yourself taking actions that do harm to someone. Yet they may have been the result of very limited choices available to you. The choice made wasn't *right*, but it was the *best* that could be made; and you have to be able to say: O Lord, forgive me. I can do no other. My destiny lies in the tears of your great compassion.

Before I put an end to this letter, let me say that there is so much more to ethics than I've been able to suggest. But you know how it is when you write a letter. You sort of come up with a stream of ideas, all bouncing off each other. It's not a lecture, a book—hardly a systematic argument. It's a sharing of insights. Remember, there are many false assumptions that make us ineffective ethically. For example, just because you will often do wrong unintentionally or because you have no choice, does not mean you can decide that it doesn't matter. You are still under a mandate to those two commandments on which hang all the Law and the Prophets. The case for violat-

ing any law must be strong, and you must be con-
trite.

It is well to realize that you never find the perfect solution; there is no one right answer available; you will often make mistakes; and you share
the guilt for the wrong your corporation commits
even if you weren't directly involved. Don't
deceive yourself. Be very suspicious when you
hear yourself saying: I wouldn't ordinarily do
this, but it means a lot to my wife. Listen care-
fully when you say: in this world you have to play
the game or go hungry. That's true, of course, but
it doesn't change your responsibilities one bit. Be
suspicious when you hear yourself saying: I
would have told the boss that the product was
toxic, but he wanted the cheapest product and he
wanted it in a hurry. These "sayings" are the sign
of slavery.

The free person says: I will do my best to live
by way of the two commandments. I know I am
guilty of being a part of a system that violates
them. Forgive me! Forgive us! Give me the courage
to go on. Help me to keep a Sabbath for my conscience, for the resources that help me to dignify
the world, to raise matter to the realm of spirit.

There is a traditional prayer we don't hear too
often anymore. Listen to it! "Direct us, O Lord, in
all our doings, with thy most gracious favor, and
further us with thy continual help; that in all our
works begun, continued, and ended in thee, we
may glorify thy holy name, and finally, by thy
mercy, obtain everlasting life; through Jesus
Christ our Lord."

When all of our doings share the mind of God
as he contemplates his creation, we are delivered
from the false notion that we are not responsible

for our business. We are also raised out of our attachment to life at its lowest denomination—the sanctification of greed. We become fully human—which is what "glorifying thy holy name" really means.

Yours in Christ

"When Prayer Seems Like Wishful Thinking"

Dear Samantha,

Well, your letter gets right to the heart of the matter. You say you've stopped praying because you discovered that it was all wishful thinking. Aha! And was it? Was it wishful thinking? If it was, why should that bother you so much? Has your wishful thinking gone away just because you stopped praying?

Of course, much prayer *is* wishful thinking. If the thought occurs to you, why fight it? You are a human being, not an angel. When this thought about wishful thinking comes to you, you must learn to say to it, "What a curious thought you are! Just as I was praying, you whisper to me,

'Hey! That's just wishful thinking!' What's the matter, are you jealous because I'm praying? So don't go away, come along with me. We'll take all this wishful thinking and we'll pray together!" The point is, Samantha, an honest doubt, an honest suspicion, is a very good thing. And it's better to make a friend of it than to let it become an enemy. After all, much of life is spent in wishful thinking. Why should it not enter your prayer life, or even be the reason for it at times?

Do you think God cares that your prayer may be wishful thinking? You have to be honest. You have to start where you are. Let me tell you a story. A farmer and his wife came to the Maggid of Mezeritch. "Rebbe! We are childless. We want a son." "Very well," said the Maggid. "That will be fifty-two rubles."

The couple began to bargain. They offered twenty-six. But the Maggid wouldn't haggle. "If you want me to pray for you, that is my fee."

Finally the farmer got angry, turned to his wife and said: "Let's go home. We can do without him. We can say our own prayers and God will help us without paying fifty-two rubles!" "So be it," said the Maggid, a smile on his face.

The couple took their wishful thinking for a son—they took it to the rabbi. But it really had to become their own prayer. The rabbi taught them that he was no magician.

How serious is your wish? Let God make of it what he will. Make it part of your own prayer.

Wishful thinking! Who doesn't start there? And will we ever be rid of it? I know, I know. What you are really worried about is that you are praying to nothing, praying to someone you *wish* were there, but you rather doubt it at times. You have been raised on enough psychology to know that auto-suggestion is a highly developed human characteristic. It is true that by simple repetition of words or actions, carried on in quiet perseverance over a certain time, we can incline our wills to believe and act on the words suggested. To some extent, certainly, prayer is that kind of repetition. And it can produce results—changes in character and even in certain functions of the mind and body. This is a case of subconscious will exerted over mind and body. In this thinking, there is no God who answers. The prayer and the answer come from a kind of hidden preserve of our own selfhood. So, if we take seriously the notions of auto-suggestion, prayer is a form of wishful thinking that produces certain results.

Now, an important thing to remember is that this psychological play is itself a form of autosuggestion. That is to say, someone who believes that all thoughts and actions are measurable and accessible to the explanations of scientific method is projecting these expectations into an imaginary situation in order to get what the subconscious will desires. In most instances, the person who is fascinated by the explanation of prayer as autosuggestion is not one who engages in any kind of disciplined prayer life. Wouldn't it be very interesting if such a person came to our Lord and said, "Lord, teach me to pray"? What would happen?

Many years ago, when I first read the words of mystics like Meister Eckhart, Jan Van Ruysbroeck, Jacob Boehme, and St. Teresa, I thought to myself, "Well, some of it is poetic, kind of beautiful; but what does it all mean?' In St. Teresa's *Life*, she writes: "One night, when I was so unwell that I meant to excuse myself from mental prayer, I took a rosary, so as to occupy myself in vocal prayer, trying not to be recollected in mind, though, as I was in an oratory, I was recollected to all outward appearance. But, when the Lord wills it otherwise, such efforts are of little avail. I had been in that condition only a very short time when there came to me a spiritual impulse of such vehemence that resistance to it was impossible. I thought I was being carried up to Heaven: the first persons I saw there were my father and mother, and such great things happened in so short a time—no longer than it would take to repeat an *Ave Maria*—that I was completely lost to myself, and thought it far too great a favour....

"With the progress of time, the Lord continued to show me further great secrets: sometimes He does so still. The soul may wish to see more than is pictured to it, but there is no way in which it may do so, nor is it possible that it should; and so I never on any occasion saw more than the Lord was pleased to show me....I wish I could give a description of at least the smallest part of what I learned, but, when I try to discover a way of doing so, I find it impossible; for, while the light we see here and that other light are both light, there is no comparison between the two and the brightness of the sun seems quite dull if compared with the other. In short, however skillful the imagination may be, it will not succeed in picturing or describing what that light is like, nor a single one of those things which I learned from the Lord with a joy so sovereign as to be indescribable."[†]

Or take these words of Thomas Traherne, written in that terrible period of English history, the middle of the seventeenth century: "You never enjoy the world aright, till you so love the beauty of enjoying it, that you are covetous and earnest to persuade others to enjoy it....The world is a mirror of infinite beauty, yet no man sees it. It is a Temple of Majesty, yet no man regards it. It is the Paradise of God. It is more to man since he is fallen than it was before. It is the place of Angels and the Gate of Heaven. When Jacob waked out of his dream, he said, "God is here and I wist it not. How dreadful is this place! This is none other than the House of God, and the Gate of Heaven."[††]

Now, I ask you: what are the options? You can say to yourself, "Hey! this person is a weirdo! He must've been 'on' something!" Or you can dismiss the whole business—the babbling nonsense of a poet of sorts. Or you can say, "I guess people used to talk like that in the olden days." And, I suppose most of us think in those ways about such writings as these. I used to. Then one day the thought came to me: what if these writers were honest, reliable people? What if they knew whereof they spoke? What if they knew something I don't know? If a discipline of prayer had

---

[†] *The Autobiography of St. Teresa of Avila*, trans. E. Allison Peers (Garden City, NY: Doubleday, 1960), pp. 360-361.

[††] Thomas Traherne, *Centuries* (Wilton, CT: Morehouse-Barlow, 1986), p. 15.

so transformed their minds that they perceived what is not ordinarily available to the mind, then—and this is a tough one, Samantha—then I can't understand or judge what they are saying unless, I, too, am possessed by that same mind of Christ that may emerge from the discipline of prayer. In which case, the psychologists who interprets prayer as mere autosuggestion are being unscientific and don't know what they're talking about unless they honestly engage in the discipline of prayer themselves—or take seriously the observations of others who are engaged in that discipline.

And did you know that this insight has very dramatic implications for our understanding of New Testament writing? Take, for example, the Gospel according to Matthew. It begins with an interesting sequence. First, the genealogy, then the birth of Jesus. Then Jesus is baptized by John. In the course of his baptism, Jesus is suddenly aware of the fact that his life is God's life, that he must claim nothing for himself, but help all people to see that they, too, are more than their own private desires. They, too, must lose their ordinary selves in order to discover new selves as children of God. After his baptism, Jesus goes up into the mountains to have his great bout with prayer. His mind is on God, but Satan keeps telling him, "Hey! Use this God-power of yours to make a better world!" God will make the better world, is Jesus's answer; God will do it if you resist the temptation to demand your own prospectus.

Then Jesus begins to go among the people, in their synagogues and in the streets. He says some unusual things: "You have heard that it was said,

'You shall not kill; and whoever kills shall be liable to judgment.' But I say to you that every one who is angry with his brother shall be liable to judgment....If your right eye causes you to sin, pluck it out and throw it away; it is better that you lose one of your members than that your body be thrown into hell."

Now, those words, you see, are the words of a transformed mind, a mind that has been disciplined by prayer. What if they can only be understood by other transformed minds—or by minds that are receptive to the possibility of transformation? Then, when you pick up those words and read them without the discipline of prayer, they will be meaningless and you will be able to do *nothing* with them. They are works meant for the mind of a disciple.

Have you ever had the strange sensation of sitting in a chair, perhaps reading or just sort of idle non-thinking? Suddenly you realize that for a split second you were in a kind of dream world, another world entirely. You may have drifted off for just a fraction of a second, yet in that blinkage a whole plot had unfolded. For a moment you're not sure what it was that happened. The plot of that tiny other world and the ordinary world about you seem one and the same. Recently I was reading some biographical reflections of the psychiatrist—the mad psychiatrist—R. D. Laing. Writing about growing up in England in the '30s and '40s, Laing says, " Those were the days of coal fires, draughty windows and doors. Every evening every winter, after piano practice, work and some reading for fun, I would curl up in front of the fire and gaze into it for half an hour or so before going to bed.

"As I looked at the fire I became absorbed in it and faded away into it. I was wide awake. It was not the same as going to sleep. I took it as much for granted as going to sleep. I could equally say I took sleep as much for granted as gazing-into-the-fire. Years later I was very surprised to find that this process, this fading away awake through empty-minded, bare attention is a widely cultivated form of meditation."[†]

What I hear Laing suggesting is that the world around is a fragile affair, filled with tiny surprises, so much larger, greater, than it seems. You see only a fraction of it at any one time. What if prayer and meditation represent a use of the mind that can reduce it to emptiness or fill it with powerful sights?

Milton Erickson, a famous psychiatrist, once asked for a volunteer for an experiment in what he called "interpersonal induction." A young man came up and sat down. Erickson asked him to put his hands on his knees. Then he asked, "Would you be willing to continue to see your hands on your knees?" The young man said he would. Erickson continued to talk to him while he gestured to a colleague on the other side of the young man. The colleague lifted up the young man's arm and it remained in the air. Erickson asked him, "How many hands do you have?" "Two, of course," was the answer. "Will you please count them as I point to them?" asked Erickson. "Certainly," came

---

[†] R. D. Laing, *Wisdom, Madness, And Folly* (New York: McGraw-Hill, 1985), p. 47.

the reply, a bit patronizing in tone. Erickson pointed to the hand on one knee. The young man said, "One." Erickson pointed to the other knee (where, you remember, the young man had agreed to see his hand), and the young man said, "Two." Then Erickson pointed to the hand up in the air. The young man stared at it, very puzzled. "How do you explain that other hand?" asked Erickson. "I don't know," replied the young man. "I guess I should be in a circus."

"That puzzle turns in on itself," says R.D. Laing. "How can we tell when, or if, we might not be enveloped in a trance, a spell, an enchantment, a dream, some blindness we are blind to, an ignorance we ignore? How can one see into, see through, fathom or wake up, or be sure one is awake?"[†]

Now, Samantha, I raise this point for only one reason: prayer may be a very simple and natural action of human beings, but when you begin to understand what's going on, you are heading into a great mystery. A mystery of the mind. A mystery of the cosmos.

When R. D. Laing spoke of "gazing-into-the-fire," what he also called "fading away awake through empty-minded, bare attention," I thought of those very famous lines that end Dylan Thomas's story, "A Child's Christmas in Wales." You probably know them:

[†] *Ibid.*, pp. 71-72.

> Looking through my bedroom window, out into the moonlight and the unending smoke-coloured snow, I could see the lights in the windows of all the other houses on our hill and hear the music rising from them up the long, steadily falling night. I turned the gas down, I got into bed. I said some words to the close and holy darkness, and then I slept.[†]

I first became aware of those lines in the 1960s, in the harlequin days when it was a joyful aim to trample the face of all that had ever been considered holy and find glory in the colors of a billboard, the label on a can of soup, or an ad for sun-tan lotion. Those were the days when the democratic spirit was fulfilled, when everything noble was levelled in the mud, and the ugly was raised to glory. I enjoyed those days, with a certain reserve. I thought they were liberating. They were the days when *Time* magazine went in mourning for one issue, with its black cover edged in red, asking, "Is God Dead?" So to read Thomas's words in those days was to lapse into a grim and devious despair—"I said some words to the close and holy darkness, and then I slept." What else could it mean? Prayer is just some words tossed into the empty *darkness.* That's all.

But now, Samantha, now I read those words differently. The words are sent into the *close* and *holy* darkness. I know now, deep in my soul, that whatever else prayer is, it is words that enter the embrace of a darkness that is both warm and

[†] Dylan Thomas, *A Child's Christmas in Wales* (New York: New Directions, 1959), n.p.

threatening, a darkness close in, filled with a certain awe. Why not? Why should it not be so? At the edge of God, it is dark!

Walter Hilton's *Scale of Perfection* is a 14th-century masterpiece of spiritual writing that influenced many later spiritual writers. "The opening of the spiritual eyes," he wrote, "is a glowing darkness and rich nothingness." The *Cloud of Unknowing* was another spiritual classic of the same century, and together with Hilton's *Scale of Perfection* and Julian of Norwich's *Showings*, sums up the great tradition of medieval English spirituality. The anonymous author of the *Cloud* wrote that in the beginning of the work of contemplation, "it is usual to feel nothing but a kind of darkness about your mind, or as it were, a *cloud of unknowing*....But learn to be at home in this darkness. Return to it as often as you can....For if, in this life, you hope to feel and see God as he is in himself it must be within this darkness and this cloud."

I think a child comes naturally into that darkness, but as she grows older she isn't so close to it as she once was. She no longer remembers the close and holy darkness of the womb, and forgets to return to it. When you pray, you are remembering that close and holy darkness, and that is good.

I read recently a biography of Iulia de Beausobre, Russian expatriate and victim of Soviet persecution, who shared her spiritual journey in several books written while living in England. Her biographer tells us that Iulia as a child used to lie awake at night, waiting calmly, expectantly, "at the edge of an unattainable expanse of darkness."[†]

That darkness is like an extension of our humanity. Somehow in the evolution of the human race, there emerged the consciousness of selfhood. Somehow in the intricate scheme that binds the darkness before time to the growing light and the green lifeline of trees and flowers, the fish who left his tailprints on the sands learned to kiss, to bark, and to howl and roar. He slithered and prowled through countless forests and scaled the sacred heights of mountains that bathed in the sun and pointed to the moon. Then at some mysterious confluence of unranked time—perhaps suddenly—the creature awoke! His grunts and groanings echoed in his skull. His eyes beheld another of his kind, and the sounds in his skull were not his own emissions. This other was indeed an "other," and he, too, was an "other." He was "I" and the other was "you" or "her."

"And God said, 'Let us make man in our image, after our likeness.'...So God created man in his own image, in the image of God he created him; male and female he created them." And this image was conscious of the fact that it was an image of something ultimate, an image toward which the whole creation pointed and in which it shared. It was an image of the fact that all creation is complete only as it points beyond itself. The

[†] Constance Babington-Smith, *Julia de Beausobre: A Russian Christian in the West* (London: Darton Longman & Todd, 1978), p. 12.

image was conscious of its share in the heartbeat of the universe. The image could pray! Prayer is an extension of the creative action of evolution itself. Prayer is the human being expressing the fact that being a person ultimately means belonging to an "other." Human existence is fulfilled in prayer. Prayer is sometimes hard to do; but in the scheme of things, in the scheme of unrebellious humanity, prayer is as natural and necessary as eating and sleeping. Only the individual who turns his selfhood in upon itself refuses to pray. To refuse to pray is to claim that the self is sufficient unto its own narrow vision. It is to thwart the evolution of existence.

Every act of prayer is an expression of the divine image at work in you, calling the image to live up to its likeness. There are two modes of prayer: the prayer of the singular other, and the prayer of common otherness. In more accustomed language, there is (so-called) private prayer and there is common prayer, but in reality there is no private prayer. Every prayer, uttered or breathed by a singular other like you or me—every such prayer is a reaching out. Whether my prayer petitions the heavens for healing, or intercedes for the life of a loved one, or sings in joyful gratitude for frogs, and rippling streams, and humming-birds, it is a reaching out in incompleteness to touch the hem of God's garment.

How can we nourish prayer as a "reaching out," an extension of our humanity? Is it possible to awaken the soul, the mind that recognizes the "creating voice" and is drawn to answer? May it not be true that the person who is agitated over the reality of prayer is already being urged by that creating voice? Perhaps the answer, the way to respond, is by way of that tradition called the prayer of the heart. The prayer of the heart is a matter of rhythm, wherein your life begins to beat in harmony with the heart of the universe. But the prayer of the heart is a dangerous affair, perhaps not for everyone. If you want to know what it is, I suggest you read J. D. Salinger's novel, *Franny and Zooey*, or the little book mentioned in the Salinger novel, called *The Way of a Pilgrim*, written by an anonymous author sometime in the middle of the nineteenth century.

"The idea," says Zooey to his mother, Mrs. Glass, "is that sooner or later, completely on its own, the prayer moves from the lips and the head down to a center in the heart and becomes an automatic function in the person, right along with the heartbeat. And then, after a time, once the prayer *is* automatic in the heart, the person is supposed to enter into the so-called reality of things."[†]

The masters tell us that this prayer should not be entered into lightly. It must begin under careful guidance and direction.

So you see, Samantha, there is a lot more to prayer than you suppose. And whether the prayer is private or the common prayer of the liturgy, it is an expression of the fact that all existence coinheres in the image of God, the mind of Christ.

It's often said that one of the lowest forms of prayer is the foxhole prayer. This is the prayer of

---

[†] J. D. Salinger, *Franny and Zooey* (New York: Bantam Books, 1972), p. 113.

a person at the end of his tether. He has nowhere else to turn. He's miserable physically, or threatened with extinction. The terror or the pain are too much. Who of us has not done that— prayed when we would not *ordinarily* pray? We think of God when we are completely up against it. How true!

During the early days of the Bolshevik revolution in Russia, there was a great deal of ugliness and violence. Many people were under the suspicion of the revolutionaries. They were imprisoned, harshly treated. Iulia de Beausobre was one of those victims. While in prison she faced her sinister interrogator—"The Snake" he was called, a hypnotic examiner with glassy white-grey eyes. She had spent weeks in Lubyanka Prison, with little to eat and hardly any sleep, what with a bright light bulb blazing down upon her in her cell at night.

"I think we will keep you here for life...Mad people sometimes reveal quite a lot about what is floating round them in the minds of others."

"Iulia's heart fluttered wildly. 'Oh, do not forsake me, Thou ...' she prayed, and the answer was simultaneous: 'Peace, child, peace.'"

A foxhole prayer, I suppose, except that Iulia had already begun the discipline of constant prayer. Earlier, when her husband was in prison and she had been forced into cramped living-quarters and constant torment, there had been a moment when she had suddenly stopped trembling. Enough! she said. We are being destroyed! Enough!

"With my last unspoken words still drumming in my mind, I sustained a great thump below the nape of my neck and stumbled forward. As I righted myself the unspoken words of Another rang through me: 'Of course it's of no earthly use to any one of you. It can only cripple your bodies and twist your souls. But I will share in every last one of your burdens as they cripple and twist you. In the blending heart of compassion I will know the full horror of your deliberate destruction by men of your own race. I will know the weight of your load through carrying it alongside of you but with an understanding greater than yours can be. I want to carry it, I need to know it. Because of my Incarnation and your baptism, there is no other way—*if you agree.*' "[†]

That is the prayer of extremity. And whether it is the foxhole prayer of the superstitious hedonist or the gracious prayer of Iulia de Beausobre, it is a recognition that there is nowhere else to turn, that you have been living as if you were complete unto yourself when you aren't. The day when you recognize your weakness and inadequacy, that is the beginning of prayer, the possibility of prayer. Ah, the possibility! Then the real hurdles begin. Very often you will discover only the darkness, the absence of God. Can you pray through it?

"The day when God is absent, when he is silent—that is the [real] beginning of prayer," writes Archbishop Anthony Bloom. "Not when we have a lot to say, but when we say to God, 'I can't

[†] Babington-Smith, p. 26-27.

live without you, why are you so cruel, so silent?'
This knowledge that we must find or die—that
makes us break through to the place where we are
in the Presence. If we listen to what our hearts
know of love and longing and are never afraid of
despair, we find that victory is always there the
other side of it."[†]

Remember this, Samantha, there is more to
prayer than this world dreams. And there are
guides to help you, to teach you, in this most
human of all human activities. This most
dignified and integral movement of human personality. Promise me that you will never give up
on prayer, or write it off because you can't find
an answer or are dissatisfied. Promise me you'll
never give it up without giving a good teacher a
chance to guide you. Promise that you will begin
a discipline of prayer, a method of prayer. Always
there are three levels of prayer. "Low prayer" is
the casual prayer before a shrine, crossing
oneself before an important meeting, or prayer
for the benefit of the self. And that is good. But
don't let it go on by itself. "Middle prayer" is
prayer for others, whether it is done in the Prayers of the People or by lighting a candle. But there
is also "high prayer," highly evolved, transformed, that loves God for God's sake and the
world for God's sake.

After all, prayer is never really (even on the
level of low prayer), never *really* the same thing

[†] Anthony Bloom, *Beginning to Pray* (New York: Paulist Press, 1970),
xvii.

as asking Mommy or Daddy for a new bicycle. It is an attitude, an atmosphere, in which things happen. There is that famous story, told by Elie Wiesel, about the great Baal Shem Tov. Whenever he saw impending disaster facing his people, he would go to a certain place in the forest, light a fire, and say a special prayer. Misfortune would be averted. A miracle, you say.

Later, when the successor to the Baal Shem Tov, the famous Maggid of Mezeritch, was faced with disaster, he would go to the same place in the forest and say: "Master of the Universe, listen! I do not know how to light the fire, but I remembered the place, and I can still say the prayer." Again, a miracle! Misfortune averted.

In another generation there was Moshe-Leib of Sassov. In order to save his people once more, he went into the forest: "Master of the Universe! I don't know how to light the fire and I can't remember the prayer. But I know this place and this must be sufficient." And it was sufficient. The miracle was accomplished.

Then came the days of Israel of Rizhin. Disaster threatened his people. He sat in his armchair, his head in his hands. "Oh, Master of the Universe. I am unable to light the fire and I don't know the prayer. I can't even remember the place in the forest. All I can do is tell you this story, and this must be sufficient." And it was sufficient.[†]

[†] Adapted from Wiesel, *Souls on Fire*, pp. 167-68.

You see, Samantha, it's not necessarily the words. It's the context—the ambiance—of prayer that counts. Just knowing the story that includes the prayer is good enough—even if the prayer is wishful thinking.

Yours in Christ

"When Money Seems to Talk Too Much"

Dear Granville,

You *are* in a fix! What is a junior warden supposed to do when pledging season comes around and the rector breaks open the homiletical files on stewardship? There's not a great deal of new material there. Sometimes it's downright embarrassing to sit there and listen to it all. He tells you you're not really giving anything because it all belongs to God anyhow. And you're wondering: well, if that's the case, then why not stick to God's distribution system? *You* know that it all belongs to God, but Toyota and Marshall Fields and Sony and Macintosh have all convinced you that what you have is necessary to their well-being, especially because their welfare is directed at giving you what you want. And if it all belongs to God—how is that an argument for pledging more to St. Woebegone's?

Of course, there are more stops to be pulled. There's the parable of the talents. Somehow it gets used to tell people not to bury their talents, but to invest them for the kingdom. The exposition then gets twisted into an admonition about your investment in the church. God wants you to show your fidelity and your investment savvy by a substantial increase in giving to the parish.

Then there's the tedious tactic of the three T's: time, talent, and, oh yes, treasure! It's been around so long! Why don't they take it out of the files? God (read St. Woebegone's) wants you to give of your whole self. At stewardship time they tell you it's not good to think that all that's being asked of you is to give money. You must pledge of your time, your talent, *and* your treasure. When you fill out your card, spend as much prayerful consideration of the time and the talent columns as of your financial support. After all, we are all ministers, not just those under the professional dispatch of holy orders. All ministers together. What is the measure of your dedication to the ministry?

The people listen and then they think: That's right, we're all ministers! The priests and the deacons are no closer to the kingdom than the rest of us. That's right! Now, what do we do? And aren't we paying those priests and that education director pretty handsome salaries? What're they trying to do—get paid for shifting the work in our direction? I have my own job and things are not too secure these days. I have to keep one step ahead of the competition and that means long hours. And we all know that clergy keep the really important decisions and jobs for themselves anyhow.

Oh, I know what you mean, Granville. I've been embarrassed listening to these programmed ploys from national headquarters that the clergy have allowed to become Gospel. We hear them so much that we begin to assume they're inevitable. And if we're honest, we will admit they have a certain phoniness about them.

But I know that some of the priests aren't embarrassed at all. They believe what they're saying. They've bought the whole file! They've become very pious pitchmen (pitchpersons?). Their intensity increases as they inform us that the tithe is the standard of giving for the Episcopal Church, by official action of the—what was it?—General Convention, House of Bishops, National Council? And why, we may wonder, was it necessary for the church to take some magisterial stand on behalf of tithing? Whether the tithe is valid theology is one thing. I'll come back to that. However, out of respect for your uneasiness, Granville, I have to tell you that I think the reasons for the renewed emphasis are tinged with anxiety.

We live in a time when " conservative churches are growing." They grow because they provide people with clear and unconditional beliefs and make a considerable demand for the support of believers. Here is no *lex orandi, lex credendi!* Oh no, the admonition is unconditional: believe this, or you're damned! Make this degree of commitment or you're an unworthy camp follower instead of a disciple!

Well, perhaps. Perhaps! But what are churches of the middle way supposed to do? We are losing ground, aren't we? We had best take thought for tomorrow, what we shall eat, what we shall drink. Hadn't we? If we don't, we may not exist tomorrow. The clergy may not be fed, clothed, and housed. The buildings of St. Woebegone's may rot in the swamps out of sheer neglect and lack of money. What better way to gain support than to make giving a fully righteous act.

What? You don't tithe? Why, that's the least you can do. There must be something wrong with your commitment. Perhaps you aren't grateful enough for what you are, what you have—*for being alive!* Remember the rich man, who "feasted sumptuously every day" while "Lazarus, full of sores...desired to be fed with what fell from the rich man's table." Remember the man who ran up to Jesus: "Good Teacher, what must I do—how do I gain eternal life?" Wasn't he told that he had to sell what he had, give it to the poor? Here we have sound basis for a strong program of stewardship. Or do we?

Well, I don't know that I can spend a great deal of time refuting that kind of theology (if that's what it is). But I can tell you that I don't think those passages have anything to do with giving to the church, or even with solving the problem of the poor, for that matter. They have to do with attachment! The rich man in both stories is a person who has stopped being a really creative person. He is attached to his possessions as the justification for his existence. He is a consumer who is being consumed instead of a creator who is in process of creation. The consumer lives by bread alone; he is so attached to bread that he sees nothing else. "Bread alone" is the rich man in Hades in torment, with no one to turn to.

"Bread alone" is *being alone.* "Death by bread alone," writes Dorothee Soelle in a little collection of meditations by that title, "means being alone and then wanting to be left alone; being friendless, yet distrusting and despising others..."[†] I suppose it's no accident of language that in our society we speak of money as bread. Like...you got any *bread*, man?

One of my favorite twentieth-century writers— I don't know whether I should call him a theologian...Correction—I would call him a theologian, but he was never in the forefront, never in the heaviest ranks. He wasn't an academic, but he was certainly a Christian intellectual. Bernard Iddings Bell—theologian, preacher, whom *Time* magazine, in the 1940s called a "brilliant maverick Episcopalian." Bell has a little essay on "The Problem of Wealth."

Poverty, he writes, comes from privilege, from "the cornering of economic advantage. Privilege is used to build up enormous fortunes that are used not nearly so much for purchase of 'good living' for the owners as in maintaining artificial controls over the processes of production and so over the lives of other people....*Privilege* is what makes poverty, not the well-clad bodies of the affluent, their too-full stomachs and their padded houses. These may be very bad indeed, but not

---

[†] Dorothee Soelle, *Death by Bread Alone* (Philadelphia: Fortress Press, 1978), pp. 3-4.

because their maintenance makes the poor poor or keeps them so....The evil of riches is...that those who possess or seek to possess almost invariably overvalue possessions and so cease to live creatively....The aim of most of our people is not any longer to be creative for the sake of creativity, but for the sake of that which creativity may produce for the creators to hold and enjoy."[†]

The "privilege" that Bernard Iddings Bell pointed to is now, a half-century later, a fact of our existence. Our economy operates on privilege. Ours is a world of investment, and investment living is nothing more than the manipulation of privilege. Thousands of wealthy people, with no interest whatsoever in creating anything—that is, anything other than money itself as a means of controlling people. The whole business is an ugly mess, leaving waste strewn by the wayside. Wasted bodies, worn and homeless. Abandoned shells of downtown stores. Empty shopping centers, hastily done as tax write-offs and investments—the ghosts of privilege.

A few years ago, when I visited Japan on my sabbatical, I was surprised at what I saw. Oh, I was intrigued by the country. But I had imagined a tidy world, sacred in its orderliness. And much of it was exactly that way. However, Japan, as everyone knows, has become a very affluent nation. Along the hedges by the sides of the streets in the large cities I saw unbelievable litter. I

[†] Bernard Iddings Bell, *God Is Not Dead* (New York: Harper & Brothers, 1945), pp. 86-87.

mean, cups and cans, wrappers and napkins, boxes and bags. And, in the parks, ravens staked their claim to territories surrounding huge wire waste receptacles, overflowing onto the grass and the sidewalks. It was very disheartening to me. Litter! Plastic bags, aluminum cans! Styrofoam! All of it the deadly residue of privilege and its greedy servant, consumption. All of it an exploitation of human weakness by an economic and political theology inherited from America. Sorry! Didn't mean to get that far into it.

In a way, this is a difficult time for the churches because they've been very privileged in America. We may have avoided making any law respecting an establishment of religion, but America relied very heavily on the churches to provide us with the convictions that were essential to our well-being as a people. We really were a Christian nation. The churches enjoyed privilege; they possessed a spiritual wealth which they shared with the country so that America was "a nation with the soul of a church." But it was privilege, nevertheless. And now the privilege is gone and the church must learn to be creative without power—its symbols ignored, transformed into secular trivia, or torn from public view by the American Civil Liberties Union.

Much of our concern for stewardship and evangelism is a matter of anxiety over our loss of privilege. The church is anxious about tomorrow, what it will eat, what it will drink. Perhaps the time has come when the priesthood can no longer be a profession—in the sense of "occupation." The time of testing is upon us. Is the priesthood always, and of necessity, a "profession" whose incumbents can command comfortable salaries in a marketplace society? Or must priests earn most of their living at other tasks?

I know you probably don't like what I'm saying, Granville. You have a fairly traditional understanding of the clergy as parson, the person/parson set aside to represent the sacred, the person who exists as the extension of the human conscience. The parson's life is not supposed to be like the lives of the rest of us—the priest does our religion for us. I can be wrong, of course, but I think the time of the parson is past and the church will have to learn what priesthood really is. Many of those who celebrate the sacraments will be people who earn their living as all people must. Their sacerdotal priesthood will emerge out of the priesthood of the church as the whole people of God. Perhaps the offices of priest, preacher, and theologian will become entirely separate.

I seem to be saying things that serve to ease the consciences of those who give meager offerings to the church while they spend untold amounts on boats, recreational vehicles, and vacations that aren't vacations at all, merely occasions of meaningless expenditure. Many people find themselves "touring" Europe, Japan, Southeast Asia, without any real interest in the cultures and people they visit. They are merely spending money and time as part of the ritual of retirement. I have no reason to give comfort to people who coddle themselves because they think they've earned it.

What concerns me very much, however, is the piety that we attach to money in American Christianity. In Europe and the British Isles the church has had an established status. Where there is an establishment, it is assumed that the church plays a public role in the society and culture. Therefore, the church is publicly supported by taxes or what may be called "livings"—incomes from endowments, investments, or land values. In those circumstances the "giving" of the people to the church tends to be either very purposeful or benevolent. You "give" to fix the roof or the pipe organ; or you "give" for the relief of the poor. "Giving" itself does not acquire the programmatic and pious intensity it has had to achieve in the American system of churchmanship.

The contrast reminds me a bit of the story of the Japanese monk, Tetsugen, who wanted to publish translations of the Buddhist scriptures, which at the time had only been available in Chinese. The translations were to be printed with wood blocks in an edition of seven thousand copies. An exhausting and expensive enterprise, as you can imagine. So Tetsugen began to travel and collect donations for the project. Sometimes people saw the value of the undertaking and gave him a few hundred pieces of gold. Most of the time he received a few coins. But Tetsugen was equally grateful to each donor. After ten years he had collected enough to begin the work.

About that time the Uji River overflowed its banks, crops were ruined, and famine resulted. Tetsugen took his project monies and helped the starving people, and then he began seeking donations again.

A few years later there was an epidemic that swept through the country, and Tetsugen used whatever he had collected for his books to help the sick and the families of the bereaved.

A third time he began collecting and after twenty years his task was completed. It's possible to see the printing blocks of that first edition of the sutras in the Obaku monastery in Kyoto. The Japanese tell their children that Tetsugen made three sets of sutras, and that the first two invisible sets are greater than the third.

It seems to me the giving relied upon by Tetsugen was either the random giving of people or the purposeful giving of those who recognized a worthy project. Tetsugen certainly recognized the value of giving; and as a monk, he knew that begging itself was an important spiritual discipline. But the people who were the givers were not monks and Tetsugen did not lay any guilt trip upon them. He thanked his donors equally. And he realized that money was only money; books of sutras were only books of sutras. The needs of people were the most essential reason for giving. Tetsugen was not attached to his project or to the giving. Giving is giving. It is not a righteous act. It just *is*.

In Thomas Merton's *The Sign of Jonas* he wrote of a day in February when the overcast skies were broken by "tall streamers of sunlight coming down in a fan over the bare hills" of the monastery fields in Gethsemane, Kentucky. The pasture was full of birds and an eagle soared overhead while the crows kept their distance high above the scene. Suddenly "a hawk came down like a bullet, and shot straight into the middle of the starlings just as they were getting off the ground." The hawk got his talons into one of the birds and soon he was all alone in the pasture, possessing his prey. The hawk stayed in the field like a king; he did not fly away like a thief. Merton thought of the flight of that hawk, the sure aim of its attack. "In the end," said Merton, "I think that hawk is to be studied by saints and contemplatives; because he knows his business. I wish I knew my business as well as he does his."[†]

We must do what we have to do. We give or we ask people to give because that is our business, but we shouldn't be attached to it. It should be a fact of existence. If we gather the funds to print the Scriptures, that is good. It just is. But if someone needs the money to keep from starving, we make another collection.

In America, however, the churches have had to be successful, competitive institutions. We have become very attached to the importance of giving. It has become a matter of life or death— for the institution and the livelihood of its "professionals." That has transformed giving into a righteous act in which we try to make Mammon act like God. We begin to serve Mammon and pretend we are serving God. But Mammon just is. I wish we could get to the point where we could act in the family of God, the household of faith, as we act in our natural families. That is, with regard to money, to finances.

In the modern family, money is a fact. In earlier times, money wasn't so important. What was important was enough to eat, enough to drink, a roof over your head, and enough to get the children started on their own. So okay. You raise a

---

[†] Thomas Merton, *The Sign of Jonas* (New York: Harcourt Brace Jovanovich, 1981), p. 275.

little wheat, some rice; you stomp a few grapes—make a little wine. You feed the cow and you milk her. Raise a few chickens, gather the eggs. You trade off some of the excess for salt, sugar. The rest is divided—some for taxes, some to barter for another strip of land, and some of it to keep the church going. Everyone has a job to do, but it's all for the community, the family. What must be done, must be done. All citizens know their business, like the hawk. No frills, no sentimental appeals, no effusiveness for doing what must be done.

But, of course, somewhere along the line the folks at the temple began to be anxious about tomorrow. They became attached to what they were doing and they rationalized it all by saying that God was more pleased with what people did as givers-to-the-temple than with what they did as laborers, teachers, farmers, creators. So they invented the tithe. But still, you know, the tithe is the product of a simple society, an agrarian and pastoral society that relies on crops and sheep and some fowl. Some of it to consume, some to trade, some to offer as a sacrifice to the God who makes crops grow and animals mate and give birth. Such a God gets hungrier and hungrier. He requires a tithe. Crops and animals are a wealth that can be shared. They can be eaten or stored. But they are used, consumed.

However, a world that lives by coin and currency is a very different world. Money is not to be shared, but possessed. It is not directly consumed, but becomes a plaything, granting the illusion of wealth. The other day I was listening to a radio talk show. The topic for discussion was welfare and taxation. One of the callers said something like this: "I resent the government taking my money for this, that, and the other thing. Giving it to people who won't work, don't deserve it."

Now, I ask you, Granville, is it possible for people in our society to believe that this "money" they "earn" is really theirs? The crops I raise, the animals I feed—they are more nearly "mine." But a coin and currency world is an intricate illusion. We can earn big salaries and cash in bonds and stocks only because we are all bound together in the vast network of corporate pretense. My $60,000 salary is not really my own; I did not really "earn" it. It is merely one of the rules by which we all play. The whole business is an inter-dependent game of illusion. It can only work if we spend and consume. I can only earn $60,000 if the government can distribute some of it and more of it is redistributed among other corporate ghosts.

We have to live in such a world. There is no other for us. The model for giving in a coin and currency world is not a tithe of one's income. The model is functional, distributive. There are no crops and animals to share. There are simply things that need doing. Tetsugen roams among us, asking for donations, endowments. He tells us he has a worthy project that requires support—he wants to publish the sutras, which contain wisdom that the world should not forget. Some people will give just because they have a few extra coins or because they can't turn anyone away. Others will give because they know how worthy the project is. They may even endow the enterprise.

We are in an age when much of the world doesn't give a damn for what we in the church teach, for what we represent. They don't care for our sutras. And many who do care have only a vague notion of what they mean. Our first responsibility in this age is the preservation of wisdom and of the tradition that bears it. But it must be a preservation without attachment. We should not cling to anything as if it could save us—not to Prayer Books, liturgies, stained-glass windows, or clerical collars. Yet all those things are important. They are Tetugen's sutras that must be preserved.

The church's business in our time is the preservation and publishing of the tradition. We must go about collecting funds for our project. Yet if at any time we must give up everything we've collected because people are in need, so be it. We are something like the synagogues in the time of exile and the destruction of the Temple. They nurtured the scriptures, the story of why this people Israel was different from other people. They kept the heritage of the Torah and raised up rabbis to interpret it. The synagogue preserved the way of the Jews, the Torah. It was like Tetsugen's sutra project.

Now, I don't know how all of this adds up. Of one thing I'm convinced: we must eliminate the sense of righteousness we attach to giving. It must be a free act. There must be freedom to give, freedom to receive, and freedom for the gift to be diverted to a greater need. Once we acknowledge that the worldly success of churches and their clergy is not essential to the kingdom of God, once we are willing to accept death, we shall be free. Money is simply money—the fact of life in a consumer-ridden world. We have to do what we can to overcome our American attachment to successful clergy and churches. It could be that a deeper spirituality exists in the lands behind what was once the Iron Curtain than what is present in America today. In those lands the church has had to die in order to rise again.

So what are the rules? First, we must go begging with Tetsugen. Many outsiders and passersby will drop their spare coins into our baskets. Some of them will do so because they patronize us, others because they want to get rid of us, still others out of sheer habit or feelings of guilt. We accept what they give. The Unification Church is a good teacher here. They raise all kinds of money by confronting the public with the opportunity to give. The beggar learns something of the meaning of life. He also learns not to be attached to his success. He learns to do what he has to do. The project is supported.

Second, we learn to give in order to fix the roof, support the priesthood, and make possible the publishing of our message. How important is that to you? Bear in mind that your giving has nothing to do with your salvation. It is what you as a human being must do, as simple as that. And you must expect no guarantees. After all, your gift may disappear tomorrow—someone may be hungry. And you will simply have to give again.

It happens all the time in the life of a family. And that's what we are in the church—the household of God. Every family has its generous people, its pinch-pennies. Every family has those who are very conscious of the love they give and the love they receive. But there are always those who just never think about it. There are those who seem to serve a private agenda. But all are members of the household. All will give at the right time. All belong together. The love that one member is conscious of is a love that all share. No one deserves it more than another. Giving just is. It is just necessary. It always happens, one way or another.

Yours in Christ

"When You Think
'When You're Dead,
You're Dead'"

Dear Larry,

My father always used to say the same thing. "When you're dead, you're dead!" He believed it! I think he lived under the oppressive weight of that conviction. Right up to the end! There was for him a flaming sign, white-hot—before which all existence, the whole dream and drama of the cosmos drifted. The sign read: Terminal! It is in death as it has been in life!

But when you think those words—or say them—it can mean at least two things. You can mean, there is no hope and life is a meaningless charade, or you can mean, death is a very real event and it represents the terminus of life as we

145

know it. Now, it seems to me that you can accept the second of the two options without accepting the first. "When you're dead, you're dead" could be a very godly thought. It could be the mind of Christ moving you to accept the fact that the life that is seeking immortality must die. In other words, when the Gospel says, "He who would save his life shall lose it and he who loses his life for my sake, will save it,"—when it says those words, it suggests that the struggle to hang on to the consciousness of the private self is a terminal affair. When you're dead, you're dead. This little "you - I" is a fragile, illusory thing indeed. There is no point in clinging to anything conceivable, because that is clinging to this body of death. This body dies, and if there is any hope, it is not to be found in the possible resuscitation of this body of death. When you're dead, you're dead. It seems like a harsh statement. But it's a good one.

This means that death is not falling asleep, nor is it entering a tunnel and coming out in the light at the other end. People may have those experiences. They may have those visions, those convictions. They may be experiences of the natural self, experiences within nature, perhaps the hallucinatory aspects of the dying experience of the private self, clinging to its visions. These experiences are very interesting. There may be many things going on in the midst of, even *after*, the experience of *dying*. But all that has to do with *dying*. We may *experience dying*, but we never experience *death*. Death is beyond experience. I think there are many experiences associated with dying that we don't understand. The reporting of near-death experiences is fascinating. And perhaps we should take more seriously than we do the accounts in which people speak of the "presence" of someone who has died.

Many years ago, in a little town in central Pennsylvania, there lived a gracious elderly woman whom I used to visit. She was a staunch Anglo-Catholic from Maryland's eastern shore, a real Prayer Book Catholic who read her daily offices and lived with the Holy Eucharist even though it was often difficult for her to find a priest of the church. She was very intelligent, highly cultured, and very devout. Her husband had died some years before I got to know her, and she lived alone on the first floor of the home she once had shared with him. Often when I visited her she would speak about her husband's presence, about how and when he came to her in her loneliness. I don't know about such things, but I take seriously people like that old friend.

And I ask: who knows what death is? Who knows when it will happen? Who knows how long it takes to die? Is it hours? Weeks? Months? Years? The people in most of the other cultures in this world seem to know the answer better than we do in the West—in Euro-America.

In Japan it takes forty-nine days for an individual to gain even partial incorporation into the ranks of the dead, and during that time the survivors are also between worlds. There are certain rituals and taboos which place the survivors and the deceased in a kind of shared realm of transition. After thirty-three years the deceased becomes an ancestor, but even then, the family do not lose contact. What is death? It is certainly not just what a physician is able to read on some life-support mechanism. Yet it is very real. And we should not suppose that evidence of the *process* of dying (like seeing light or having a feeling of benevolence) is hope for escaping death. The self must die; that is the soul of all high religion.

There is a Sufi story which is a favorite of mine. The last time I told it, the people sitting around the table said, " So what?" But then, they were a rather rationalist cadre of academic priests. Let's see what happens when I tell it to you. It seems that the Mulla Nasrudin needed a big cooking pot to prepare for his daughter's wedding. He went to a neighbor and asked to borrow one. Now, you know you have to be a very good neighbor to lend a big cooking pot. The neighbor was reluctant.

" Only for a week!" said the Mulla. " There are so many people to feed. My good friend, please help me out." " All right! But only for a week," said the neighbor.

Well, how surprised he was at the end of the week when Nasrudin appeared on his doorstep with the pot. He lifted the lid, and inside was a little pot.

" What is this?" asked the neighbor in amazement. " I'm very happy to tell you," said the Mulla, " that while your pot was at my house, it had a baby!" " Marvelous!" said the man. " Marvelous indeed!" And shaking his head in bewilderment, he carried both pots into his kitchen.

About a month later, Mulla Masrudin again stood at the man's door and asked for the loan of the pot. " My wife's family are visiting," he started to explain. But the neighbor stopped him, " Say no more, my dear friend. You took such good care of my pot the last time you borrowed it that I don't hesitate for one minute! Here, take it!" So Nasrudin left very happily, carrying the big cooking pot.

A week passed. Two weeks. Was it a month? No sign of Mulla or the return of the pot. Finally one day they met on the street. "My pot, Mulla. Where is my pot?" asked the neighbor.

Mulla Nasrudin began to shake his head sadly. "I'm very sorry. I have put off being the bearer of sad tidings. I regret to say that while your pot was at my house, it died."

"Nonsense!" shouted the neighbor. "What do you take me for? How can a pot die?"

"Well," replied Nasrudin, raising his hands in a gesture of helplessness, "if a pot can have a baby, surely a pot can die!"

So what do you make of the story, Larry? Do you say, "So what?" Contrary to the sentiment of my friends who sat around the table and listened to my story of the pot that died, I don't believe that "So what?" is a very good theological question. Next time they say "So what?" I'll just tell the story over again. It's easy for the mind to accept the product of the imagination when it benefits us, not so easy to accept something detrimental. Perhaps pots do not give birth or die, but if you live in a world where pots can have babies, you live in a world where pots can die. You can't delude yourself. You can't have things the way you want them, not when it comes to matters of life and death.

Death is very real and very final. The early Christian community, the apostles, the followers of Christ—they were not believers in tunnel experiences or immortality of the soul. They accepted the fact of death. The faith of a

Christ-follower begins with the acceptance of death. In many of the old Benedictine monasteries there were chambers of skeletons that the monks contemplated. It sounds morbid, but it probably wasn't at all. In fifteenth-century Japan there was a Zen monk by the name of Ikky. "To the eye of illusion," he wrote, "it appears that though the body dies, the soul does not. This is a terrible mistake. The enlightened man declares that both perish together."[†]

Nothing that Ikky says is contrary to the Christian way. The notion of a soul that survives the death of the body is not a Christian notion, but a Greek one, the scholars tell us. You may have heard it before that the word for soul in Greek is *psyche*, the same word that is used for butterfly. In Greek thought, the body was a prison for the soul, a kind of cocoon from which the "butterfly" escaped. All of which meant that the very word "soul" implied some kind of entity that survived the body.

But the Jews understood life as a totality of body and soul, of flesh and anima. They lived together. They died together. "To the eye of illusion, it appears that though the body dies, the soul does not." If a pot can have a baby, a pot can die. Now, I happen to think that much of Buddhist thought about the nature of reality is a better vehicle to interpret the Christian way than are most Greek and Western metaphysics. In Ikky's time

[†] In Frederick Franck, ed., *The Buddha Eye* (New York: Crossroad, 1982), p. 84.

the city of Kyoto with its palaces and temples was reduced to ashes. Many people had to flee to the countryside for refuge. There were fires, hunger, disease, and the world was a place of corpses and skeletons. Ikky wrote about this world and his book came to have the title *Ikky's Skeletons.*

" I came to a small lonely temple," he wrote. " It was evening, when dew and tears wet one's sleeves, and I was looking here and there for a place to sleep, but there was none. It was far from the highway, at the foot of a mountain, what seemed a Samdhi Plain. Graves were many, and from behind the Buddha Hall there appeared a most miserable-looking skeleton, which uttered the following words: 'The autumn wind has begun to blow in this world; should the pampas grass invite me, I will go to the moor, I will go to the mountain. What to do with the mind of a man who should purify himself within the black garment, but simply passes life by.'

" All things must at some time become nought, that is, return to their original reality. When we sit facing the wall doing *zazen*, we realize that none of the thoughts that arise in our minds, as a result of karma, [is] real. The Buddha's fifty years of teaching are meaningless. The mistake comes from not knowing what the mind is. Musing that few indeed experience this agony, I entered the Buddha Hall and spent the night there, feeling more lonely than usual, and being unable to sleep. Towards dawn, I dozed off, and in my dream I went to the back of the temple, where many skeletons were assembled, each moving in his own special way just as [sic] they did in life. While I marveled at the sight, one of the skeletons approached me and said: 'Memories there are

none: When they depart, all is a dream; my life—
how sad! If Buddhism is divided into Gods and
Buddhas; how can one enter the Way of Truth?
For as long as you breathe a mere breath of air, a
dead body at the side of the road seems something apart from you.'

"Well, we enjoyed ourselves together, the
skeleton and I, and that illusive mind which
generally separates us from others gradually left
me. The skeleton that had accompanied me all
this while possessed the mind that renounces the
world and seeks for truth. Dwelling on the water-
shed of things, he passed from shallow to deep,
and made me realize the origin of my own mind.
What was in my ears was the sighing of the wind
in the pine trees; what shone in my eyes was the
moon that enlightened my pillow.

"But when is it not a dream? Who is not a
skeleton? It is just because human beings are
covered with skins of varying colors that sexual
passion between men and women comes to exist?
When the breathing stops and the skin of the
body is broken there is no more form, no higher
and lower. You must realize that what we now
have and touch as we stand here is the skin
covering our skeleton."[†]

I suggest to you, Larry, that Ikky is not a morbid person. He is a happy person, an enlightened
one. To see the skeleton is a very profound and
necessary "happening"—I don't want to call it an
"experience" because that isn't a word I find par-

[†] *Ibid.*, pp. 77-78.

ticularly helpful. An "experience" is usually something we think of "having"—sort of the posses-
sion of the individual self. What we are talking
about here is an occasion in which the individual
self is *transcended*—"lost" in the Christian sense.
Ikky has discovered the coinherence of all things.
It is an amazing discovery. Suddenly there is
nothing to prove, nothing to defend. The skeleton
is a very interesting visitor. "We *enjoyed ourselves together*," said Ikky, "and that illusive mind
which generally separates us from others gradually left me." The skeleton confronts us with the
reality of death but in the process we discover
that neither life nor death is what we ordinarily
think of it.

"When you're dead, you're dead," is a good
beginning on the road to salvation. What have I
said thus far, Larry? For one thing, that death and
dying are two different realities. Dying may be a
long-term process, one that begins even before
the vital signs begin to go. It may last well beyond the measured end of vital signs. I don't
know. Certainly not all the people who report out-
of-body experiences, or rendezvous with ghosts
and spirit forms—certainly they aren't all neu-
rotic or credulous. But death itself. That's another
matter. Death is a visit with Ikky's skeletons. It is
a spiritual reality as well as a physical one.

You see, death is the end of what we ordinarily
know. Death is the end of every form of existence. Everything that˜*is* issues forth out of emptiness. Out of nothing.

I hold a flower in my hand. It is the Holy Scriptures of the New Covenant, the pages of the Revised Standard Version. The teaching of Martin
Luther, of Thomas Aquinas, of Richard Hooker or

St. Ignatius, in which the mind of Christ is presented to the world—they *are* this flower. These petals, this gentle scent and the smudges of pollen—this flower. The teaching, the Gospel, are not something you can hold, or keep. Nor is the flower.

All things come out of the emptiness. The genius of Einstein, the successes of Lee Iacocca—out of emptiness! The African daisies in the late winter, the poppies of spring on the desert, the snows of winter—all of it out of emptiness. All is without beginning, all must end. All of it together is the vast sea of coinherence. Suddenly, all is beautiful. Each is beautiful. And even on the vast sea there are ripples. The ripples are the personality of God, the cresting, pulsating of the heart of the universe.

And that personality is itself a gift of perception, because it is a person that is doing the seeing. It's good science to understand that perception is always dependent upon the instrument of perception. Personality perceives person, at those moments of perfect freedom when I accept death and see the emptiness out of which everything comes and returns. Person is born out of nothing. The mind of Christ.

I'm sorry, Larry. This has gotten a bit onto the " heavy" side of things. It all depends upon how deep you're ready to go. I think you should know this at least: there's always more depth than you've ever yet been able to plumb. I'm certain of that. Just as I'm certain that death is a reality that must be faced, and when you face it, then death also is somehow devoid of reality. That's because the reality of death is still part of the thinking of the private and sensate self who has not yet become person.

Face up to the reality of death. So what shall we do? We must *prepare* for death. In his autobiographical memoir, Eric Hoffer tells us that by the end of 1931 he had made up his mind to commit suicide because he had no intention of becoming a prisoner of jobs in order to subsist.

" 'What could it matter whether I died at the end of this year or ten years later?' he asked himself. On the morning of what he assumed was to be his last day, he was beset with a 'dark worry hammering' on his brain. 'It was not the fact that I was to die in the evening,' he wrote, 'for death had no image or voice which on closer approach I could see or hear and be gripped with fear. Even as late as the small hours of the preceding night my mind was peaceful. I was rereading for hours the tales of Jacob and his sons, chuckling over the vivid details and marvelling at the unsurpassed storytelling. Now I was like one lost in a dark forest; I dared not leave my bed....In retrospect, it is clear that the reason for the sudden worry that morning was simply the disappearance of a tomorrow. Death would have no terror were it to come a month from now, a week, or even a day. For death's one terror is that it has no tomorrow.'"[1]

No tomorrow? Is that it? It's not death itself that's worrisome. It's dying. It's all that realization that there is no tomorrow, no anticipation. I

[1] Hoffer, *Truth Imagined*, p. 23.

remember that Carl Jung said somewhere that his research indicated that the loss of tomorrow is the beginning of death. He discovered in his aging patients that those who didn't look forward to the next day became disabled, moribund, morose. We must prepare to die! When we do, we'll not be concerned about death. We will already have accepted it and every tomorrow becomes a gift.

In Peter Matthiessen's book *The Snow Leopard*, he tells about his long and dangerous journey into the high Himalayas in search of the snow leopard. He is in the land of the great mysteries of Tibetan Buddhism. There are many hazardous ledges to traverse, in which one false step could mean the end. He notices that one of his fellow pilgrims seems very casual on the ledges: " The telescope strapped across his rucksack, caught upon a rock, could nudge him off the edge; I can scarcely look. However, I am getting hardened: I walk lighter, stumble less, with more spring in leg and lung, keeping my center of gravity deep in the belly, and letting the center 'see.' At these times, I am free of vertigo, even in dangerous places; my feet move naturally to firm footholds, and I flow. But sometimes for a day or more, I lose this feel of things, my breath is high up in my chest, and then I cling to the cliff edge as to life itself. And of course it is this clinging, the tightness of panic, that gets people killed: 'to

clutch,' in ancient Egyptian, 'to clutch the mountain,' in Assyrian, were euphemisms that signified
'to die.'"[†]

I think what Matthiessen is talking about is
"letting go," accepting death. He speaks of keeping his "center" of gravity in the belly, of letting
the center "see." It means he has discovered a
way to allow his existence to move with the
"Tao," the Word, that is the eternal flow of emptiness out of which everything emerges. When that
happens the self has stopped clinging to its need
for preservation. The self "lets go" and we partici-
pate in the dramas of selfhood and personality
going on all around us. His feet begin to move
naturally, thinking for themselves, because they
are no longer the slaves of a self that is afraid to
die. Matthiessen, in that account of *The Snow
Leopard,* was intoning a constant prayer that has
the effect of transcending all forms of attachment
to things or to self. He was learning to let go, a
kind of practice of death.

Tibetan Buddhism speaks of Bardo—a state be-
tween-two-existences, a kind of dream state. The
Tibetan *Book of the Dead* contains instructions for
passing through that dream-state of Bardo. The
teaching is that a person's last thoughts will de-
termine the quality of his reincarnation. Therefore, every moment of life is a preparation for
death. Every moment is to be lived as if it were
the last. One prepares for death by learning to let

[†] Peter Matthiessen, *The Snow Leopard* (New York: Bantam Books,
1978, 1981), pp. 134-35.

go, to live only in compassion for all of the suffering creatures of existence. Now there are distinctively Christian ways to handle this same discipline, this same way of living. The Tibetans live life in preparation for death; so should Christians. The person who learns to let go by preparing for death will live life to its fullest because her center is not the self; rather the center of the universe has occupied the center of her life.

Paul Tillich used to speak of the "courage *to be*." It's not always easy to understand what he meant, but he said that courage was "the self-affirmation of being in spite of the fact of nonbeing...[an] act of the individual self in taking the anxiety of nonbeing upon itself by affirming itself either as part of an embracing whole or in its individual selfhood." That sounds as though the options are pantheistic absorption of the self, on the one hand, or some form of egoism on the other. I haven't been talking about either of those options. There is no *self*-affirmation. That is a form of clinging or clutching. Nor is there an absorption. Rather there is the discovery of "person" that is greater than the self to which we cling. That discovery of "person" takes place as the self accepts its death.

There is one final thought to share in this letter. I feel very strongly about the fact that we need to find greater means for ritual participation in the experience of death. We've allowed the technological society to rob us of our freedom in death. Technology dictates to us what death is. But technology doesn't *know*. It can never know. Technology says that death is the end of vital signs. Burn the body or bury it. That's it. The funeral industry tells us how to take care of this business—how much to spend and how to conduct the services. But the funeral directors don't know what death is. To them it is a once-in-a-lifetime deal. Embroider it with sickening flower scents and organ tremolos.

I'm glad that the church has begun to reassert itself in these matters. There are canons concerning the proper farewells for a Christian. "Baptized Christians are properly buried from the Church," says the Book of Common Prayer. "The service should be held at a time when the congregation has opportunity to be present. The coffin is to be closed before the service, and it remains closed thereafter. It is appropriate that it be covered with a pall or other suitable covering." The point is that death is understood in a certain way by those who belong to the one, holy, catholic and apostolic church. The Christian lives and dies in the body of Christ, not as the world lives and dies. We must accept any discipline offered that helps to express that perception of the world.

I have some close friends who now live in the Southwest. Our friendship is older than a quarter of a century, and when I first got to know them, back in Pennsylvania, they were dedicated and informed members of the Presbyterian Church. The husband was a Presbyterian clergyman. They had two children, raised in the church and provided with good educations. The couple are now divorced. Both are remarried. The woman and her new husband live several hundred miles from us. We see them occasionally. Recently we had a letter that read: "We have been studying Buddhism for ten months and been inspired by both Sarah's and Kevin's involvement with NSA. I know there is a large group and community center in Phoenix."

Sarah and Kevin are the children, neither of whom lives with Betty and Walter. When I received that letter I couldn't believe it. Sarah and Kevin were involved with NSA, and Betty and Walter had been studying Nichiren Buddhism for ten months!

NSA is Nichiren Shoshu of America. That's a form of sectarian Buddhism. Now, I study Buddhism too and have a great deal of admiration for it. But I don't study it with the thought that I might join some Buddhist movement. Why, I wondered? Why would people who have been privileged and educated members of the Christian church find it necessary to turn to Buddhism?

Well, I don't have time to go into the particularities of Nichiren Shoshu. But one thing stands out in my mind. There is in this tradition the practice of regular prayer, disciplined prayer, that always acknowledges continuity with a reality beyond life and death. Prayer is the prayer of the "communion of saints." Every member of NSA has a lifetime loan of a Gohonzon, a mandala enshrined in a box-like wooden altar. Daily worship consists in reciting certain chapters of the Lotus Sutra, five times in the morning and three times in the evening, followed by chanting the Daimoku, Nam Myoho Renge Kyo—"Hail to the marvelous teaching in the Book of the Lotus Flower." Now, that comes from an old Buddhist practice of daily chanting before the *butsudan*, the home altar.

I think we Catholic Christians need to set up home altars again. I think we should have candles and crucifixes. Every individual should say prayers from the Book of Common Prayer before the altar daily. Those prayers should be memorial prayers in which the deceased members of the family are prayed *for*; and prayed *with*—we should pray *with* them. We should develop chants and prayers that tie us together in the great bond of the communion of the saints, across the boundaries of life and death, across the years. We should ask the priests for regular visits to our homes for the chanting of psalms and the saying of special prayers for the departed.

The Orthodox Jews have three successive periods of mourning. What makes us think we have been released from the need to observe times of mourning? Why does no one say *kaddish* for me when I am gone? What kind of a family is this? What kind of a church, in which we are terminally separated from those who belong to us even in death? Why are our liturgical practices associated with death so final? Where are the memorial masses of our forebears? Is the church not part of Israel, the people of God through all generations? Why do we not restore the practice of All Saints Days and All Soul's Days? We *can* when people like you, Larry, begin to ask for it because you know that the meaning of death and resurrection is something we must preserve. The alternative is loss of our freedom, captivity in the deathfulness of a world in bondage.

Yours in Christ